Laney Pemberton & Tyff Gomery

# Life Hurts
## But Only
# Sometimes

A TRUE LIFE STORY

novum pro

This book is also
available as
e-book.

www.novum-publishing.co.uk

© 2017 novum publishing

ISBN 978-3-99048-826-3
Editing: Rachel Jones, BA (Hons)
Cover photo:
Viachaslau Rutkouski | Dreamstime.com
Cover design, layout & typesetting:
novum publishing

**www.novum-publishing.co.uk**

# Contents

# Dedications

This book is dedicated to the many people who helped me on the road to recovery from a Chrysalis into a Butterfly. Without the individuals who gave their help willingly and for free, I would not have reached the pathway of success I find myself on today. June Axon and Susan Bean encouraged me throughout my journey. They are still with me today as valuable friends.

I literally owe my life to these individuals who remain consistent in their commitment to others and their plights. To my dearest Dad, Mum and brothers whose support has been a great strength to me and their unconditional love instrumental in my growth, development and recovery.

To Dennis, for his support and trust in me at a time when I needed friends and to be believed. To Laney Pemberton for her support and belief in me and for writing the book with me.

To the various counsellors and societies that helped with the domestic violence and support needed. They helped me with the steps for change and an altered attitude.

I also dedicate this book to all those who have been or are in an abusive relationship. By reading this you may get an insight into what makes a narcissist/sociopath tick. For those of you who are still struggling, there is a way out I promise you.

All the names of the characters involved in my life during these times have been changed to protect the authors and those individuals who have helped me on my journey.

I dedicate this book to all who have suffered abuse or are still in abusive relationships; to let you know there is a way out and I pray that you find your way to a peaceful, loving and happy life.

You will find in life that abuse attracts abuse, to change your life you have to send out to the universe happiness. Happiness attracts happiness, like attracts like, gratitude attracts gratitude, love attracts more love, positivity attracts positivity and negativity just brings in more negativity.

I changed my thoughts to ones of loving gratitude and appreciation of all that was good in my life and did not focus on what wasn't.

It is a positive move for you to change the way you feel, think and speak and try not to use the words don't, no, can't.

If you tell the universe that you don't want abuse you will receive more of the same. Change it and say that you want a healthy, happy relationship with lots of love and you want harmonious and peaceful surroundings to live in.

I used the law of attraction to change my life so I bought a book and film. I focused on the principles of them both and changed my life. I also used the daily teachings to enforce this positivity into my life every single day.

CHAPTER 1

# The Road to Recovery

My life today is not what I had expected it to be and there has been a complete transformation of my mind, body and soul. To arrive at where I am today has taken enormous courage and strength. I have been to hell and back over the past thirty years. Life hurts but only sometimes I used to tell myself. I never thought that I could have or would have been an alcoholic you never know what life has in store for you or what the next day will bring. There have been some good times but mostly not and I never found the inner peace that I yearned for. The only peace I found was in the first few years of my marriage to Anthony, now my ex-husband. They were the happiest and seem so distant now. During the last three and a half years I have remarkably been reborn in all areas of my life and I am astounded by my own transformation. From being down and out and a drunk not far from the gutter. I had gone into Manchester City centre for a date and he had taken me to a pub where I had a glass of wine. We had some lunch and then I started to chat about what his hobbies were and I was completely taken aback when he said his main hobby was something that he did on his own. I thought to myself what does he mean as there are loads of hobbies that you can do on your own. He then went on to elaborate about his hobby which basically was relieving himself. I sat there and didn't know what to say I didn't know whether to laugh or cry. I thought to myself *how have I ended up here?* I once lived in a lovely house with my family and great career and now I'm sat here with a pervert. I excused myself saying I was going to the loo. However, I made a quick exit out of the rear door and headed towards the bus stop. I was so shocked and traumatised I went and bought a bottle of wine and drank it at the bus stop.

I am now a Complimentary Therapist. I have my own home and car with a new career which I absolutely love. I studied hard to re-train as a complimentary therapist securing a Level 3 Diploma. I was absolutely ecstatic with my results and gaining a first in this diploma lifted my spirits to new highs. I also attended an alcohol and drug team to enable me to recover from alcohol dependency; some might say I am now a recovering alcoholic. I became a recovery champion and subsequently obtained a role as a volunteer where I helped other women and men who had suffered similar circumstances, physical and mental abuse, to find their way back to a normal life again and into recovery. The majority of the work was about recovery and about me telling my history of violence and abuse. My own path to recovery started after I had left my ex-husband and had to move in with my mum; no choice, as I had been locked out of my own house. During the time at my mums I experienced what is called A Dark Night of The Soul. Where I confronted my inner most fears. I felt I was facing a life or death situation in my life. I asked myself whether it was worth living or not. I was in bed under the covers with no light in the room; the curtains were closed and it was terrifying for me as all my fears came alive as if real. This Dark Night of the Soul is an old Egyptian initiation where the High Priestess/or High Priest would be put in a sarcophagus for several days with no light and just enough air to breath so as not to suffocate and if you were still alive after two to three days you had passed. In this situation you would feel totally alone and would have to face all your worst fears. I felt that I didn't fit into this world and was all alone and felt completely misunderstood. I felt everyone viewed me as this evil person. When we face this in our real lives a lot of people don't survive, they commit suicide. My type of suicide was alcohol, a very slow painful death which totally consumes us. If you survive the Dark Night of the Soul it can lift your whole life to a higher and clearer level. This can happen when you least expect it. It can be triggered by deep and dark emotions that surface. It can also serve like a healing and useful function if we face the deep and dark emotions. Nearly all our behavioural patterns are triggered from something that happened in our childhood. So when you get very painful feelings just ask what they are here to teach you. Ultimately, it will boil down to the very simple process of forgiving yourself and those that have caused the pain but not their actions. Always stand up for yourself and never put up with any form of abuse.

My road to recovery was very long, very hard and full of obstacles, the majority of which were caused by my ex-husband as a sadistic way to bring about the maximum amount of pain that it was possible for him to inflict on me. His lies, deceit, and torment became apparent as the days went on. The lies unfolded when my mind became more focused and much clearer about what had actually taken place over the years of my marriage but especially the last year. The clarity brought the truth and a great sadness to me to learn that the two people I had helped most in their lives were the two people I could actually trust the least and had planned to destroy me. The betrayal was like a pain searing through my heart. I just found it so hard to believe that these two people could have plotted so hard to bring about my demise. My friend thought she would get my husband and my home and my husband thought he would get my home too. These two Judas's were my ex-husband Anthony and the other was my friend Katherine. We had been friends for over twenty years, and I had trusted her with my life. I had helped her in many ways throughout the extent of our friendship which I was happy and quite willing to do. A major mistake on my part. I gave unconditional love to both Katherine and Anthony and had also saved Katherine's life when she was in bed vomiting everywhere, not very pleasant I might add, after a night out of hard drinking. We were both drinking but she had drunk a considerable amount more than me. She was choking on her vomit so I had to put her in the recovery position and stayed up all night to ensure she didn't choke and was safe. I will go into this friendship and what led me down the pathway of self-destruction further on. She actually tried to encourage me to drink during this period making it so very hard for me. What kind of person would encourage a friend to drink when they know it is dangerous for them and that they shouldn't be drinking to that extent? What kind of person would leave a friend, who was in a dangerous condition through alcohol abuse and was hallucinating, on their own to perhaps choke on their vomit or just die? Well that's exactly what Katherine did to me. She left me in a desperate condition and didn't even call an ambulance or get help, she just left.

I left my home in November 2012 and I saw Katherine several times up until the 23rd January 2013. I met up with her, and another woman who was a friend of ours, on the 22nd January 2013. We were having a drink and something to eat. Katherine mentioned something quite relevant (a filing cabinet) and this seemed strange to me. This devastated me immediately because she wasn't able to find anything at work she lost everything and was so disorganised. She said she had been out and bought this filing cabinet. I didn't believe her as there is no way that she would have done this. She lived in total chaos and she had a filing cabinet. Her sports bag was full of old banana skins it was disgusting. She was so tight she always got men to buy her presents and pay her bills. Why would this be strange you may ask, well because my ex-husband bought me a filing cabinet saying it was to organise me. I desperately needed to go home to my mum's house as I was so devastated by this revelation and of course I drank to drown my sorrows. Didn't I always!! I thought hard about what she had said and this was the first twist in the tale that led me to later believe it was her having an affair with my husband.

Whilst I was at my mum's house and still drinking on and off, something quite profound happened to me when I was in my bedroom. I hadn't had a drink for several days and I turned and looked to the left hand side of my bedroom where there was a picture on the wall. The picture wasn't of my dad but his face was projected onto it. It was quite a large image and very much larger than the picture itself. I stared at his image in disbelief and not quite sure what was happening. I closed my eyes and looked again and I knew that I was clear of mind at that point and I managed to click him out of my mind quite quickly as my dad died four years earlier and I had never seen him before. I am positive that he knew how bad my mental state was at that point in time and how low I had sunk and he came to reassure me. I know that's what it was. About three days after that event I was in bed crying feeling bad about the end of my marriage and taking the blame myself. That was what I used to do. As I was always blamed for everything that went wrong by Anthony. I was lying in the foetal position on my left side and I felt someone rubbing softly along the top of my arm. I felt this fairly solid touch as if there was someone in the room sitting beside me trying to reassure me. I looked around the room and there was nobody there. It had startled me a little but I did feel though this was my dad trying to reassure me again. I have no doubt now in my mind that this was my dad coming to comfort me in the darkest moments of my life. I felt uplifted by this and it gave me the hope I desperately needed to move forward. You see I had become a hopeless drunk as it numbed the pain of the constant abuse over a prolonged period.

The thought that Dad was here looking after me was so uplifting and such a comfort to me. I chuckled to myself as Dad was a chocoholic and used to have a stash hidden away as Mum was very careful with how much he could have. She tried very hard to keep Dad going for ever but unfortunately he passed over when he was ninety years old. He was a very wise man. I was very grateful and very lucky to be his daughter. He also had a really dry sense of humour and he was so funny. He was academically brilliant with three honours degrees but his favourite programmes were On the Buses, Doctor Who, and Bless This House. I think these gave him the escape he needed from his constantly thinking mind.

Three months after these two events I went with June, a friend of mine, to a Mind, Body and Spirit event in Stockport. Ali Mather was working there and she was a novice medium on the circuit and just starting out. She had been giving readings at her home but this was her first public event and I was her first customer. I had not known at that time that she was also a recovering alcoholic, having not drunk for eight years. She had also previously been in a very abusive relationship. I was eight months sober myself at this point.

As I entered the room I looked over towards her direction and she was sat on her own and for some reason I felt drawn to her. I headed straight in her direction and asked how much a sitting would cost me. She advised it was £30.00. I had no cash on me and only had my credit card but she didn't have a card machine. I felt so drawn to Ali that I asked if there was a cash machine in the vicinity. She told me where to go and as soon as I had withdrawn the cash I went straight back to her. Within minutes of us sitting together she brought my dad through, providing me with irrefutable evidence that she could not have known as we had never seen each other before. There was no one at the Mind, Body and Spirit Fair that she could know that would be able to provide any details about me and my life to date. She mentioned that my dad was telling her about him appearing over the picture on my bedroom wall and how he had been rubbing my arm to comfort me. I was astonished by this information and was really eager to hear more. She told me that I had not imagined it and that my dad had come through to me because he was very glad that I had left that man and was very proud of me. He meant my ex-husband Anthony as he would have killed me if I had stayed any longer. I had thought this of Anthony many times; one day during his beatings he would kill me. I had feared for my life on numerous occasions. She also knew all about my abusive relationship and my alcohol dependency. It was almost as if I had known her for many years and she went on to tell me about my friend, Katherine, of many years. Katherine was the one of the two people I could trust or so I thought. Ali said that in my heart of hearts I knew she was not a good person or friend and never had been. She was so right about that. So the whole discussion was taped and she went on to provide so much more evidence that I could validate and the evidence was so specific it was really uncanny. Ali told me that I had a very logical mind and that was why I had difficulty in believing it was my dad coming to me. She also told me about my son Connor who had been in-doctrinated by Anthony into believing I was a really bad moth-er. Of course, I am partly to blame as I was so bad with the al-cohol due to the abuse and he had witnessed not only the abuse but seen me drinking and Anthony had set me up for a big fall in front of Connor on numerous occasions. She went on to say that my ex-husband was like a schizophrenic in that he would show one side of his personality to my son and others and yet a different side to me. She went on to say that my son Connor would come back to me eventually but it would be a long time yet before that happened and she advised me to send him a mes-sage on Facebook to explain why I drank. Also that my dad was telling me to read a book, as my dad was a prolific reader, called the *Celestine Prophecy* which would explain what had happened to me and the reason that I was sucked dry of energy. It would also explain why I became powerless against Anthony, enabling him to control my life. My son was present throughout all of this and he therefore learned this bad behaviour too. Ali also sug-gested that I watch a film called *The Secret* and follow the prin-ciples behind it and advised that I would be on a spiritual path-way moving forward. From that day forward I began the work I needed to do to work out who I was as a person now and not the victim of Anthony that I had been for so very long. I read a great deal and researched all aspects of spirituality digesting the knowledge of many books. Some may feel this to be strange, but to me at that time it felt so right. Ali Mather is now an excellent medium hosting her own events. She is such a wonderful person.

The most important part of my recovery was to stop drinking and I went into a recovery unit, Chapman Barker in Prestwich, Manchester. They were recommended to me by the consultant on the ward who I had worked with and he was so shocked to see me as ill as I was. He held my hand whilst listening to my story and was absolutely horrified. However, what was more impor-tant to me was that he believed me and offered me a place that day to get the help I needed. I accepted the help knowing that I wasn't going to get well on my own. I owe my life to that man and I will always be truly grateful to him for his help and belief in me. I had actually worked for him for about ten years. I was admitted and was in there for a week. It was almost like being in prison (not that I have ever been to prison) with the very strict regimes and routines. There were many people in there with me from all walks of life and I was so surprised. Some were heroin addicts, alcoholics, and many with different dependencies and addictions like me struggling with one demon or another in their lives. I made a promise to myself that I would get myself better with their help and went to every single lecture and talk to inform myself and soak up any knowledge I could about my dependency, alcohol and what the affects were to those people in my life. There was one particular woman in her late twenties who inspired me so much it really hit home and I began the manifestation of recovery. Even though her own mother had just died she still came in and gave the talk about her own recovery. I thought to myself, my goodness, if she can come in and talk about her own life whilst going through bereavement then I can do this too. I made a decision at that point to never drink again and to be an inspiration myself for others to follow and I have never drunk from that day forward. It is now over two and a half years since I stopped the alcohol abuse. Occasionally I got the thought to drink but the alcohol and drug team helped with those feelings and provided the help and guidance I needed to ensure I worked through the problems that could take me from my future pathway.

From that point on I attended a society for alcoholics and I asked a woman there, who sponsored people and had helped over a hundred women on the road to sobriety, if she would help me. She had worked in this environment for over thirty years and she volunteered her services for free and is a truly wonderful woman. She is now eighty six years old and of poor health yet still always helps newcomers to the fellowship and her name is Joyce. I am truly grateful for her help and I am so very lucky to have met this earth angel as I call her. Although she could be really grumpy, she is what she is with a heart of gold. She will tell you straight and often she used to say "Shut up and listen to me". She was the expert so I did and I really wanted to know how she had done it as she had been an alcoholic up to the age of fifty-something. She turned it around and then used her experiences to benefit others. I attended the meetings regularly, followed the steps and still do to this day. I learnt about people and the types of personalities that I needed to watch out for. I therefore choose my associates and friends very carefully and listen to my gut instincts as I am no longer controlled or allow myself to be controlled by anyone. **I am now free**.

Whilst I was still working and shortly before the end of my marriage I attended a Women's Charity to gain help and understanding of how to stay in the marriage but make it better for me. I had sessions every week for weeks and weeks and I tried and tested the methods I was given, which only helped minimally. Since that time I have been visited by the Counsellor, for the Women's Charity who is willing to write up my notes, which is the evidence I need to help me prove to my son that I had gone and tried to get help for how to live in an abusive relationship as I wished it to work for my son and myself. However, it was not to be as Anthony was (I now know) a sociopath with narcissist behaviour and the violence and abuse would never stop as it was Anthony who was ill and needed help; I was just one of his victims. The others were my friend Katherine, my daughter Rachel and my son Connor. I also attended a course provided by a Women's Charity for free, for half a day a week. The course explained the tactics of the abuser. It explained how they will use any of a large variety of tactics to maintain control over the others in their lives especially those very close and they often utilise your best friends. This explained, to me, the link between abuse and substance abuse and to enable me to get into recovery I had to first understand that it wasn't actually my fault and that Anthony had tried to blame me for everything. The next step was to get off the alcohol, and as explained above I successfully achieved this. Abusers often come up with some extraordinary reasons and excuses, i.e. my friend's husband tried to get her to return to him after their break up after his numerous affairs, bullying, and intimidation, by telling her he had throat cancer. She fell for it for a week until she investigated the evidence he gave her and she found it to be false. He was just trying to ruin her new relationship and he was insanely jealous. A bit rich really coming from someone who could never keep it in his pants. Laney was a strong person and did not want him back. He even tried to get her back whilst he was still living with Diane his new partner. He attacked Laney's new partner physically but he didn't get anywhere as he had picked on the wrong man. Laney moved on with her new partner and has been in a happy relationship for nearly fifteen years now. I was not as strong as her but it wasn't a weakness it was just that my husband was a sociopath. Anthony had this superficial charm about him but underneath was a nasty conniving piece of work. He manipulated me and members of our family and was very cunning and intelligent orchestrating my demise by drink. Secretly hoping that I would kill myself and he could have the house all to himself. He had a strong sense of grandeur but he wasn't grand at all and had an overinflated ego. He could lie so convincingly and proved it because he tried to ruin my career and take my son from me and he succeeded in both. There was no empathy or compassion with him throughout all the years we were together. I had thought that he actually loved me but I eventually came to the realisation that from day one he had his own agenda set out for himself. Even though we had our son Connor he never really loved me or showed it. I suffered verbal outbursts daily and physical punishments seemed normal to him. Anthony only ever said he was sorry once, the time he threw me across the kitchen. He would often act quite strangely the following day as if nothing had happened. Even though I may have had black eyes, a split lip or gash in my head. He used to go through the motions but he was shallow and deceitful always planning, manipulating events, and acting out his role as the perpetrator. He would often be outraged by insignificant matters and would often remain unmoved and cold by what would upset a normal person. Anthony always needed stimulation and used to exercise to excess and drive himself to get a degree. He wasn't happy unless he was top dog wherever he worked. This behaviour was also used against me in the bedroom and he would never let me out of the bedroom until he had finished with me. We were in there for hours and his stamina was amazing but again he had a hidden agenda for this too. He would always insist on forcing me to stay in the bedroom for sex, quite bizarre too, on occasions, when I was supposed to be with my friends so that one by one I lost them. I was not aware of what he was doing at the time and was powerless against him.

I was so controlled and I found myself in a state of panic if I hadn't got the tea ready in time for Anthony coming home. The funny thing was that he never ever turned up on time and was always late with some feeble excuse. I would often leave the tea, put in the fridge, until he came home around nine pm. To control me and undermine me he wouldn't eat it anyway as obviously he had been somewhere else. He never ever said thank you to me for my trouble. Yet I still made his meal every night because I was too frightened of his temper and the abuse I would suffer if I didn't. I used to get into a state of panic about it. When he did eat he would sometimes play with the food, pushing it around the plate, saying "What is this rubbish?" Always undermining me and my efforts to please. In fact I could never ever please him as that is not what he wanted. The tactics of the abusive perpetrator are deliberate, which I found out from the course I went on. I also learnt that their actions are deliberate and they gain significant satisfaction from seeing their victims upset, hurt, belittled, humiliated and they take great satisfaction from this and actually like it. This was Anthony's behaviour and he blamed me for everything; not taking any responsibility for his actions but delighting in the fact that he had reduced me to a quivering wreck and dehumanising me. He had to be in control and made to feel important and welcomed to the home after work. He needed this so badly and would go out of his way to make sure he got this from me. Anthony seemed to have a very deep seated rage at his very core and it rose up through him like a volcanic eruption and culminated in a beating for me.

Part of my recovery involved learning about the type of person that my ex-husband was and how he worked to control me and to make me submissive to him at all times. Also as part of my recovery I went to a charity for women which mostly involved contact over the phone. The operator helped me by listening to me, talking with me and offering advice on how to escape from the tyranny and abuse I was suffering. She gave me a panic alarm and literature. She also contacted the fire brigade to install smoke alarms in my mum's house where I was living and a metal plate across the letterbox to prevent the abuser from torching the house. It was quite terrifying for me and my mum but it was a fact of life that some abusers go to these extremes. The women's charity helping believed that Anthony was that much of a risk to me and also to my mum for helping me.

I always remember that my dear friend and neighbour, Laney, who lived next door but one, had tried to help me over the years and witnessed violence towards me on a couple of occasions. She had tried hard to get me to phone the police but I was too frightened and therefore I didn't. She did but unfortunately got nowhere at the time. Laney told me many times that Anthony was showing behaviours of having an affair. Stupidly I told Anthony about this and he ordered me to go round to her home and tell her that he would rip her head off if she interfered again. She also thought it was quite unhealthy that my friend Katherine was at my house four to five times a week. Always turning up unannounced. You see Laney had heard on the grapevine about Katherine's reputation and furthermore she didn't like Katherine at all. Laney took little notice of what anyone else said. She had a gut feeling and actually was always right. Furthermore, Laney wasn't frightened by Anthony's threats at all and challenged him in the front garden. She was going out and was driving away from her house just passing ours when she saw Anthony washing his car in the driveway. She wound her window down and shouted to him that here she was if he wanted to rip her head off. Why didn't he come and try it. She said he was a coward and could only hit women who he had weakened and abused. He turned his head away from her and he just ignored her. I carried on working with all the support mechanisms that were now in place.

Once my family knew and were aware of what had been happening to me, they provided me with the additional support and love I desperately needed as part of my recovery.

Slowly over the past two and a half years I have come to realise that my marriage was finally over and was not real anyway – it was just an illusion provided by Anthony to get me where he wanted me to be. I actually believe he became an addiction too, strange as it may sound, as I got used to his abuse and I honestly believed at the time it was better for me at that point in my life to have a bad relationship than no relationship at all. I do believe this is true as I wanted so much for it to be right. In the early years of my marriage it was fabulous. Anthony could not do enough for me and this lasted for the first three to four years. So I found it hard to believe that he could do the things to me that he did. I had spent years and years wondering if he would ever kill me and was frightened on a daily basis. His attacks were brutal and terrifying for me and my son Connor as he had witnessed some of it. Towards the latter part of our marriage the attacks became worse, far more violent and he used to scream at me in rage whilst abusing me. I believe that Connor buried these terrible times deep down in his subconscious. Anthony had yet another victim and he totally controlled my son. My friend Katherine even witnessed one event and never did anything about it. You see she was an accomplice that ended up as his victim. That's why I could no longer trust her or him. They were both oblivious to the devastation they had caused to my family. My recovery didn't include a friendship with Anthony or Katherine.

# CHAPTER 2

# The Pathway of Trust, Deception and Lies

I first met Anthony when we were neighbours. I was with my first husband and he was with his wife at the time. They were newly married. The first meeting that I can remember with Anthony was when he was outside his house walking with his dog. He was saying that he was finding his marriage hard and that he didn't really want to be married. I thought blimey what a statement to make after only being married a short time. I remember saying to him that marriage is always difficult in the first year as you have to learn to live with someone and their behaviour but he seemed to look right through me and I remember that whilst talking to him he was pulling the dog along on its lead in quite an aggressive manner. I took no notice of this at the time. But now realise this is one of the traits that they display. I often used to go the Home Watch meetings with Anthony and he offered to be my co-ordinator and so a friendship developed at that time which was purely platonic. He then went on to have two children and my first husband and I moved to Davyhulme in Manchester. Anthony brought his wife to visit us once and saw the detached home that we lived in. There was one occasion where, my husband had left me, Anthony brought his wife over with their new son and he had told me that my husband was seeing someone else and that my husband had been to his house and told him all about it and also when they had been out for a drink together. You can imagine how I felt having this thrown at me; I was not happy about it at all. A really big confrontation then followed between myself and Anthony with him telling me that I should divorce my husband (who was no longer living with me) and I had actually moved on from this. The confrontation was about Anthony trying to impose his will on me then and he felt I shouldn't be with my husband because he had been having an affair. Anthony then left with his wife and baby after quite a bizarre afternoon -his wife having to witness the whole scenario. She didn't seem to upset by it and looked quite bemused. Anthony didn't seem to give a monkey about his wife and behaved as though he was going to rescue me from my husband. I later relented and I gave my marriage one more shot with my husband which only lasted for a month or two. I didn't really know why my husband had gone, but when he came back he said he had been having a bit of a breakdown and wanted to get back together and try again. I didn't tell him what Anthony had said about him. I eventually found out about his affair which was still carrying on and he was actually living with her on and off. I went to the car one evening and found two fancy dress outfits, one male and one female. I hadn't been invited to the company party so I knew he must be going with someone else. That evening we had a row about it I told him that I was intending to commence divorce proceedings and if he was to continue with the other woman that would be it. I had also found a solid gold bracelet in one of his tracksuit bottoms that I had washed. I mentioned this to him and he said he wanted this back because it belonged to the girl he was having the affair with. It was a present to her for her twenty first birthday from her parents. I was so angry with him I refused to give it back and gave it to my mum. She still has it to this day.

I felt this was her fault for having an affair with a man that she knew to be married with a small child. The same evening that my husband left and I threatened divorce I made a phone call to who I thought was Anthony's wife as I needed to talk to someone. I don't know why I chose her I just did. I think I had a suspicion that she had been through similar experiences from her behaviour when they came to visit that time. Anthony answered the phone and I asked to speak with his wife. Anthony told me that she did not live with him anymore and had not done so for about a year. He told me that he had moved to Moston in Manchester and bought a house with her and one day he found out she had emptied the bank account and that she had been draining it over a period of time. He only found this out because he went to buy some new clothes and he had only just been paid (he was working away at the time and earned a lot of money) so was astonished when his card was rejected. When he returned home the house had been emptied and they had all left. We talked on the phone for quite a while and I asked if there was any hope of reconciliation between them. He said she had left him several times and had been going out on Saturday evenings and not returning until late in the morning. She was always last in the taxi. I said "that's funny I'm splitting up from my husband". We talked about what I would like to do in life and then the conversation ended. I went up to bed as I was feeling really deflated at the realisation of the end of my marriage. I also had a two and a half year old daughter to look after. Anthony called me back in the early hours of the morning and I felt slightly elated as I thought it was my husband calling. I was hoping he would come back. Anthony started talking about our situations and that we were both on our own and would I like to go for a coffee with him some time. I was a little surprised as he was younger than me but I then thought oh why not I had nothing to lose and he was a friend. We were both now free to do so without incrimination. I agreed to meet up for a coffee and then to my surprise he said he would come round to my house straight away and he was there within forty five minutes. I was still in my P.J's as I did not expect him to turn up. I should have listened to my instincts that it was all happening too quickly. He was actually extremely lovely towards me, showing empathy which he could never show normally so it was obviously superficial at the time. In hindsight I believe he was interested in my home, being detached and in a really good area, I had a good job as a physiotherapist, and was well paid and respected. He must have thought he was on to a winner. Which he was as he took me for everything. Looking back I also believe he thought I would be a great asset to his future plans as he was extremely career focused, which I thought to be a little egotistical, also saying he felt that he could be capable of being the Prime Minister. I remember thinking wow he is very confident.

My job was at the Treeford General Hospital just around the corner from where I lived in. I had a responsible job and was in charge of the medical wards, neurology, and stroke patients and it was extremely demanding. I worked for six consultants within the hospital. Anne who I had worked with at a Manchester Hospital, on the neurology unit, became my true friend inside work and also occasionally outside work. This relationship developed and then she met her husband Stuart and was engaged to him within six weeks of meeting him. At that time I was still living with my ex-husband in Radcliffe and worked at Hope Hospital. I moved to Davyhulme partly because Anne lived there and because my husband at the time had friends there too. I then relocated to Treeford General Hospital. She moved to another children's hospital to work as she was a paediatric physio and I was an adult physio. We got our senior one positions on the same day. We left the Manchester Hospital on the same day. We kept in constant touch with each other because we both lived in Davyhulme. Anne often came round to my home for coffee. Anne then introduced me to her twin sister Katherine who had been through the same situation as me with her hubby having an affair and it had been painful for her when she had found out about it. She remained in their home with her young daughter who was three years old and I thought we were like kindred spirits going along the same journey but on different pathways. She used to come to see me frequently, at least a couple of times a week and I felt this was of a supportive nature towards me as she was in the same boat. She was also looking for a new man in her life and had met a man but he wasn't very well off and she seemed to want someone who had money and could support her and her daughter. She then mentioned she had met a man in a pub who she said had won the new business enterprise competition and was running his own business, however, he had a girlfriend. Somehow, she worked away at it and she ended up with Dennis who was doing really well in business and had his own house in the area. Katherine was never attracted by looks, it was the money that was a magnet to her and he was going places and he did do very well indeed securing a portfolio of rented houses etc. within the North West. He also had his own business in data cabling installations. I am trying to paint a picture of how Katherine came into my life and also the connections with my ex-husband Anthony. I wrongly assumed that they could be trusted and were reliable and honest people. I couldn't have been more wrong and that was one of the biggest mistakes I ever made.

I read this quote which goes "Truly evil people don't just hurt others they take pride in the pain they cause and then try to blame their victims". This is so true of Anthony and Katherine.

Anthony was also in the picture now. He sent flowers to my workplace, twice, which were extremely grandiose and my boss even commented that somebody really loves me now. One was four feet tall and must have cost a fortune and the other was a massive basket. I gave the basket to Anne because I couldn't take them home as my ex-husband was still coming to see our daughter and often came into the home as we didn't want our daughter to be involved in it all. Anthony took me out quite a lot and showed me a really good fun time, which I hadn't had for quite some time as my ex was too busy taking other women out. I hadn't really got over the breakdown of my first marriage when Anthony came into my life. He often took me to Moston where we started our relationship. He was in his own environment so he was in control. He was very clever how he did it and careful as not to push me towards a sexual relationship until about three months into it. We both enjoyed a drink but he especially did as he was still traumatised from the breakup of his marriage as he had told me. I left myself wide open as I had had no breathing space between the relationships. Anthony swept me of my feet and was incredibly sexual and supportive and had moved in within four months from when I first met him for coffee. He was really active in the bedroom which I remember was fantastic at the time. However, he never really found out if I was really enjoying our romps. He shagged me in every position you could think of and the intensity was mind blowing. He tried everything on me which was new and exciting and stimulating. He loved the stimulation of it all and he was very much in control. I remember thinking that he must have been around a bit as he was very knowledgeable between the sheets, on top of them, on the floor and every room in the house that he could have sex with me. It seemed to me passionate and energetic. He truly turned me on and on and on with such intensity and the orgasms were electric. I don't exaggerate when I say that we had sex all the time and many times during the day sometimes. I wanted more and more of this. My daughter was being looked after by her dad for those short periods of time that I went to meet Anthony at his house. He clearly dominated me in and out of the bedroom his knowledge was vast and yet he didn't use any sex toys or pornography. He was obsessed with sex and I believe he actually had an addiction for it and I was the addiction for a while. I was his plaything for a while. I was elated and ecstatic with the attention and felt very sexual. He made me feel like I had never felt before so clearly had me under his spell in the sex department. Once the boring stuff started to come in like making the dinner, cleaning up, etc. he quickly lost the intensity of the interest he had shown in me.

I had already organised to go on holiday to Tenerife with my mum which was originally for me and my ex-husband. I was surprised that Anthony called quite a few times on my mobile whilst I was on holiday saying how much he missed me and what he wanted to do to me in the bedroom. I was getting turned on just on the phone call. I now know he was checking on me to make sure I didn't meet anyone else. He needed to make sure that he was going to move into my home. He made sure that there was no possibility of my ex "S" coming back into my life. My daughter was about three years old at that point and he was delightful with her. He had me hooked I thought to myself how lucky am I sex on a plate whenever I want it, every move under the sun, and his own son and daughter by his previous marriage used to visit our home together for a day a week initially. Usually a Saturday or Sunday. However, it was me that had to look after both his children. I used to bath them as they were quite dirty, especially their finger nails, when they came and their nails were never cut. I think his ex-wife did this on purpose to get back at him. I didn't understand why she had left him at the time I only had his version of events. I remember her once telling me that in anger Anthony had smashed his hand through a door. I now understand he had a problem well before he met me. He also told me about his terrible upbringing and the abuse he had been subjected to by his father. He and one of his brothers had the same father while the eldest brother had a different one and he didn't seem to get any of the abuse. The two children that were naturally his father's boys were the ones that were abused. He had a sister also who was younger and from what was said to me she wasn't abused. Anthony did not see his father for the last ten years of his life nor did he see his mother for the same period. He was not told about his mother's funeral so he missed it and he did not visit her in hospital either although had the opportunity. When his mother became very ill and was in hospital I tried hard to encourage him but he refused to listen and took no notice. His elder brother phoned him several times about this. Yet I met his father right at the beginning of my relationship with Anthony we used to go to the pub with his mum and dad and a couple of other friends. Anthony frequented pubs all the time and I went with him and ended up drinking with him but never lost control at that time. The break up between his parents and himself came shortly after we returned home from a short break in Italy with Laney and Martin. His mum and dad had looked after Connor whilst we were away and upon going to pick him up on our return the change in Connor was so significant, he didn't even seem the same child. He told us about the terrible shouting and later on told me that he was underneath the kitchen table to get away from the shouting. I discussed this with Anthony and said they were never to look after Connor ever again and basically the last time we saw his Dad was many months later when Anthony had cleared out some of his shirts from the wardrobe. He told me that he was going to give them to his Dad I just sort of agreed with him and didn't think too much about it. However, he put the shirts in the boot and we were in the vicinity of his parent's home and he asked me to call them to see if they were in so he could drop the shirts off. I made the call and his Dad answered and I told him that Anthony had some shirts for him and could we call in and drop them off. His response was quite rude saying to me that they were about to have their tea. I replied it was OK we were not coming in we would just drop them off. This was not long after Christmas and Connor had not received his Christmas presents so I thought it may have been an opportunity for his grandparents to have given them to him. However, when we arrived Anthony got out of the car and went to the door whereby his Dad answered and took the shirts then closed the door. Anthony got back in the car and said what an ungrateful bastard. I just mentioned that I didn't want anything more to do with his parents and that I didn't want to call there again or for them to visit our home. We never saw them again until his Dad had died and we went to the funeral home and viewed him in his coffin. I was quite surprised as he hadn't spoken to his Dad for ten years. I remember looking at him thinking good riddance to bad rubbish. I shouldn't have felt like that but I did he was a nasty horrible man who had abused his wife and two of his children all their lives until the boys left home.

At the on start of our relationship, after he had moved in, he was very attentive often doing a lot of personal stuff, like doing my streaks in my hair. He organised me and this led to him buying me a filing cabinet. I can laugh now because it was really funny and it was a very strange present. But you see that was how his mind worked and I actually thought he may have had OCD. He talked a lot to me asking me about my previous relationships and quite in depth about my life to date. Looking back in hindsight I believe this was to find out about my strengths and weaknesses.

Anthony took me everywhere and showed me off to his friends and relatives as if I was a trophy and he kept a diary about what we did on a daily basis. (I thought this was strange really but a credit to his organisation skills.) If you read this it was always very positive about me at that time and I refer to this as love bombing.

He was sucking me in to his world and he used to be empathetic about my previous relationship and he had said to me that it was obviously not my fault. He was just saying this to suck me in further and he also said he would never do that to me, i.e. have an affair or treat me badly. The interesting thing was that he used to say to me that some men keep their diamonds at home whilst obviously sleeping with rough cuts. He portrayed himself as a very different kind of individual to who he really was. This is actually like a secret language of the sociopath which I now believe Anthony was and still is. I say this because I have researched this as part of my recovery process. What I found was these individuals walk amongst us every day often being charming and charismatic hooking in their victims. Most importantly their cruelty is deliberate and it is designed to control and ultimately destroy their victims. There is a mismatch between their words and actions. They will say one thing to you and go and do something completely different therefore confusing their victims. They consistently lay the blame at their victim's door for not only their victim's behaviour but they blame their victims for their behaviour too. Their behaviour can affect their victims for a long time after the relationship has ended. This can affect their victim leaving them with post-traumatic stress disorder which can be crippling and long lasting. These types of abusers are very dangerous with mental and physical abuse and they can attack at any moment with condescending remarks, sarcasm, verbal abuse, physical abuse and blame shifting. Whenever they perceive you as a threat or need some entertainment in the form of an emotional reaction they use non-verbal language such as a sadistic smirk or a cold deadness in their eyes whilst professing to love you. I always remember Anthony having black eyes, they were really very dark brown, but they appeared black with an evil look. He also had an evil aura around him like a cloak. A sociopath would also make you feel that you believed that you are inferior to them. They will actually bully you to death to make you feel this. They are relentless in their pursuit of what they want and they will do anything to achieve their aims. They seek to destroy you in every way possible.

There are three phases that the narcissist (which is part of the sociopath's behaviour) will use; the first one is the flaws, short comings, insecurities and secrets that you have confided to them. The second one is your strengths and accomplishments especially the ones they are pathologically envious of. The third one is your need to please them and their need to be perpetually dissatisfied with you. I identified in hindsight that he utilised my weaknesses for alcohol and the love of my daughter Rachel at that time. He drew me in initially by being superficially charming and superficially empathic. He used the initial information that he found out about me when questioning me in the initial stages of our relationship to his own goals. He made me believe that he loved me immensely in the initial stages of our relationship often taking me out for meals and totally spoiling me. He did a lot of DIY in the house showing himself to be indispensable even to the extent that in the pouring rain he would be outside stripping the paint off the windows before we had double glazing. This I found quite hilarious and bizarre. I thought to myself that he was mad and why was he doing that in the rain. Going to the extreme was often the case with him.

I invited my mum and dad for dinner one evening and my mum commented to my dad that Anthony's car was right in the middle of the drive and although it was my house, I had to park my car on the road. My mum said that they would have trouble with Anthony. She could not get over how Anthony wouldn't let me do anything in the kitchen and he was no chef at that time. She said it was over the top and couldn't believe that he had tidied the kitchen. It was spotless and it always was. He would not allow any of us to do anything. It was all a show. It was part of the process of him drawing in all my friends and family to believe that he was a fantastic guy. This was part of the scene setting, all a game, for a narcissist. They will pretend to support you and empathise with you but this is entirely superficial. They will later use this against you to provoke, belittle and demean you. These are just a few of the things he did. He was a master of disguise he was like a chameleon changing his colours to suit his needs. He took me in hook, line and sinker and all he actually wanted was the house and money. He was in admiration of my professional standing which he then, later on, completely and utterly destroyed deliberately as I wasn't doing what he wanted me to do. I was of no use to him anymore so he simply went and found other victims (other minions to manipulate against me) Katherine being one of them and the other woman from the health club. I think Katherine knew about the other woman, who was also called Katherine making it confusing but it avoided any confrontation if he slipped up with the name. I don't believe the other woman knew about my friend Katherine. This was a woman who purported to be my best friend. I will say it was extremely complicated and I will have to be careful in my writing not to confuse you the reader.

I think the best way for me to communicate this to you is to draw a diagram:

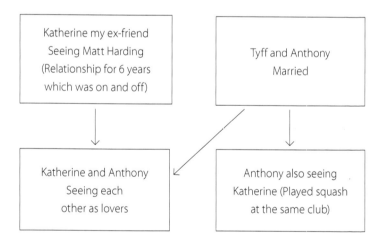

The relationship between Katherine, my ex-friend, and Matt Harding was basically a smoke screen in reality and also Anthony and Katherine (squash player) was also a smoke screen. I believe that Anthony told Katherine he was only seeing the squash player to remove any suspicion that they were having an affair. Anthony was also conning my friend Katherine as he was using her as a tool to hurt me and get rid of me. Eventually he dumped her, destroyed me and went off with the squash player. He was very clever and manipulating and always succeeded with his game playing.

I knew what was going on as I had seen Kathrine the squash player and Anthony together at the Health Club as I was there swimming with a girl called Jane Heathcliffe and I remember looking over and Anthony was talking to Kathrine and there was only inches between them. I saw them very clearly as the squash courts are all glass and he then saw me. His arm was touching her waist and he moved away very quickly. I felt very uneasy at that point. I thought to myself this is his next victim.

In October 2012, prior to the relationship ending in the November of that year, we had both gone together to a beautiful wedding in the Lake District and it was the marriage of Kathrine the squash player's ex-partner James. He was actually marrying a girl he had had an affair with previously and they now had a child who was at the wedding. Anthony was the best man at the wedding and it was a very small ceremony as they both worked for the Police as undercover agents in different countries. We all had to be CRB checked prior to the wedding. Anthony and I stayed at a bed and breakfast on the Friday evening in readiness for the wedding on the Saturday. We went to where James and his wife-to-be were staying for a meal and it was a beautiful farmhouse. The stay at the farmhouse was a wedding gift to them by their two barrister friends. It was absolutely gorgeous and was set in the most amazing countryside away from the hustle and bustle of life. James came to our little bed and breakfast to guide us to the barn to make sure we didn't get lost as it was in the middle of the Lake District. I went out with Anthony to meet James. I didn't know him very well but he came up to greet me by giving me a hug which I thought was lovely of him. It was quite strange really as I felt a sadness in him when he had hugged me and I thought to myself at the time that he knew what Anthony was up to. I had a knowing at the time of what he was thinking and feeling. Which I knew to be true later on. Anthony having two women in tow as well as me is not unusual for a narcissistic sociopath. There are no limits to what a narcissist will do to get what they want. They thrive on the fact that they are traumatising you making them feel powerful as it is the only power they have ever had in their pathetic empty lives. Any open wound in their victims is an invitation to always cut a wound even deeper. Because Anthony knew my ex-husband had an affair he would use this insecurity to damage me even more deliberately. He would rub salt in my wounds by mentioning my ex and his affair but he used it as a deliberate tool for him to dehumanise me further. It had two effects for him, one he is having a great time sleeping with someone else but using that strategy to dehumanise me. This was even more traumatic for me and satisfying for him. I hope this makes sense to you. Also to utilise my close friend Katherine in an affair would cause me even more major trauma, which it did, I was devastated by this. Katherine was also a narcissist as they were jealous and envious of me as a person. They knew I had a good reputation and she hated me at work because everybody liked me and I was a hard worker and really enjoyed my job and she wasn't, she was clever, but very manipulative and lazy. She was off sick once the same day I was off on holiday I went down to the Health Club to play tennis and I was quite surprised to see her sat there with a group of affluent ladies who all had very rich husbands. The wealthy women always played tennis on a Wednesday morning and I had gone to play tennis with them. She took a week off work pretending to be sick. When she saw me she was shocked as she thought I was at work and didn't know I had taken the day off. She actually said to me that she had felt much better that morning. I laughed inside to myself thinking just how stupid do you think I am. I knew Katherine got off on seeing married men with money and used to taunt her husband with the fact that her lover had bigger parts than him. What a callous cow I know this because he told me and I have a sworn and written statement signed by him. She totally tried to dehumanise him and humiliate him. Throughout the whole of Dennis's marriage to Katherine she was seeing her brother-in-law Stuart. His wife Anne found out about this when Dennis went round to their house to confront Stuart about underwear and strange messages that Stuart had sent to Katherine, his sister-in-law. This caused a family rift between the twin sisters and they didn't speak for over a year. Destruction followed Katherine and Anthony wherever they went. She destroyed Dennis as she was also seeing his best friend behind his back which he found out about. I knew about this as Katherine told me herself. She told me that she had been going around to Dennis's best friend's house (Luke and Bernie) to do physiotherapy on Bernie's knee replacement. This could have been unpaid I can't be sure about this. Whilst there, Katherine was making an excuse to go upstairs to the toilet whilst Luke would be waiting upstairs for her. She told me he was kissing her passionately and wanted a year out of his marriage to be with Katherine. This has been verified by Dennis her ex-husband as he witnessed them kissing at a friend's party in their swimwear. This was one of the reasons his marriage to her ended by his volition and not as she tried to claim by blaming it on him having depression. He was having depression as she was having affairs with everyone around her. What is the female version of a stud? She is what I call a pariah basically, becoming an outcast by all around her due to her behaviour. This reminds me of a scene in a funny film where one of the actresses is in conversion with her daughter and she says that she knows that this woman is a pariah. The daughter says mother do you know what a pariah is and the mother replies saying "Of course I do darling, it's a fish".

I believe I have now set the scene for you as to what was happening in my life and how humiliating I found it all. Initially Anthony put me on a pedestal making him feel superior as his origins were very different to mine. I was brought up in Marple Bridge in Cheshire and my Dad was a University Lecturer with three honours degrees. One was mechanical engineering his main career, but he also had two others in mathematics.

My Mum was a general science teacher and was brought up on a farm and went on to pass her eleven plus and go to university. A plaque was up on the school wall to say she had passed her eleven plus as most of the woman of her time became farmers wives and cooked as that is what they did in that era. Anthony's Dad was a convicted criminal who had been in prison for burglary. He was an abusive Dad and a conman just like his son Anthony. I am not making fun of him in anyway as this is a tragedy for anyone in life. They are both victims of their circumstances in a way and I find that to be very sad. Anthony thought that he was on to a good thing with my career as a senior one physiotherapist and my qualifications and on much more money than him at the time we met. I had my own house, career and car and his outlook on life was very materialistic and mine wasn't. I believed I had achieved what I wanted from my career and the material things in my life by very hard work. I believed I was very lucky and I was certainly very grateful. Once upon a time I was confident and sexy to Anthony but then in the devaluation of myself by him I was basically rubbish and fat. I was also a drunk. I decided to go on a wine diet as then you don't give a shit how fat you are. I was intelligent and driven as he described me when he first met me but now he described me as useless and unorganised slug and he made me feel inferior with his behaviour towards me. For example, I spent all morning cleaning my car and I was really pleased with the work I had done and I thought to myself yes that looks good, however, he came out and he found fault with what I had done, there was a tiny little mark on it, as the character Victor Meldrew would say "I can't believe it". He would go around the car inspecting the cleaning standards and pointing out my failures as he put it. When I was feeling really very happy with my standards. I thought my standards were normal, I was a bit untidy but was more relaxed in my approach to life in that I wanted my house to be clean and tidy but wanted a home not a show house. Whereas Anthony wanted a show house and a show woman as this uplifted his self-worth.

# CHAPTER 3

# The Abuse, destruction, and Self sabotage

A narcissist seeks to destroy their victims in every way possible so that their victims in turn destroy and sabotage themselves. All while they sit back relax and watch the unravelling of everything their victim has worked hard for and that means everything, your sexuality, your life, your money, career, family, friends and home. The narcissist will utilise anything to destroy their victim. Kathrine was his minion and was used by him and she used him too. She thought she may end up with a man with money as he was climbing the social and career ladder very fast, had his master's degree in strategic management, and was very successful. He thought that when his boss left he could take his place having achieved his degree. He also had casualties in the workplace, as one woman put in a complaint about his bullying and another woman left due to his bullying. Both these woman were at companies he had worked for. He was, however, too clever and a case could not be proven against him. He therefore actually got away with bullying these two women who unfortunately for them crossed his path.

Throughout the latter part of my marriage to Anthony I was an alcoholic but I had always been a social drinker and never really drunk too much I just had one or two glasses of wine and some fun socially. I had never lost control of my drinking until this point in my life. I only drank to excess as his control took over. Anthony progressively took over my life and took away my identity and I, believe it or not, let it happen because I could not cope anymore with my life the way it had become. There would be times when he was really nice to me and I thought, mistakenly, that it was back to how it was. What a fool I was to believe he loved me as it was complete control and abuse of power over me. It was like a war zone in our home with my daughter to my previous marriage and my son to Anthony. My daughter spending most of her time in her bedroom because she was terrified of him. Even his children from his previous marriage were subjected to abuse and power control. Only Connor escaped the violence but his mind was manipulated and towards the end it was as though he had been brainwashed. I am aware that my behaviour as a drunk would not have impressed him but I would have thought at least he may have had some love for me as his mum. Connor never showed his love towards me but treated me exactly as his Dad did with total contempt with no compassion whatsoever towards me. He did know about the abuse as he witnessed a lot of it. This has left a great sadness in my heart. The last good memory I had of my son was when I was driving to the Health Club on a Wednesday for a swim. I saw Connor walking down the road so I pulled up beside him and wound the window down. I smiled and told him that I had bought the book he wanted about a famous footballer. I also told him that there was a book signing event at the Treeford Centre the following day. He said to me on this occasion that he loved me in his head and in his heart. I thought how lovely. Anthony beat me up really badly the next day as I had seen him at the club as previously mentioned. Connor was upstairs in the bedroom and I am not aware of what he knew about this but he never again spoke to me kindly after that. This broke my heart.

The decline in my self-esteem and self-confidence was sustained over a long period of time and was continuous and aggressive. There have been hundreds of incidents where he verbally, physically, emotionally and sexually abused me. One really prolific incident was after we had been married for eighteen years and he suddenly changed his sexual preferences. He asked me if he could shave my pubic area removing all the hair. I was very vulnerable at the time and I allowed him to do it. Some women may like this but I didn't as he wanted it done for him and it was not me wanting it myself. He then went on to have mad passionate sex after seeing me like this. He really got off on it. Personally I thought myself it was unhealthy and I didn't like it and it traumatised me, but as I wanted my marriage to work I had gone along with it. At this point in my life I was so vulnerable, my self-esteem was rock bottom and he was using me as a sexual object and not as a person whom he loved and this is how I felt because it was for his own gratification and he wasn't interested in whether I was happy with it or not. On occasions I had been left feeling as thought he had raped me as I wasn't in agreement with what he was doing. I mentioned this to my friend Katherine who seemed to think this was because he was having an affair with someone else. This was during the time I thought I could trust her. There were many other occasions he used the sexual card especially on one occasion when I had arranged to meet a friend, who was previously a probation officer, and I was meeting her on a Saturday to go for a walk together. Anthony tried it on with me that Saturday morning, he never left me alone for one minute. I could not get showered and dressed to meet my friend on time. This was because he was taking me away from friends and family. She was a powerful strong woman and had a knowledge of abusive behaviour and consequently, although I had text her to explain that I would be late; she was not there upon my arrival. It was bitterly cold and she could not have waited any longer. I went to her house from the meeting point and apologised to her profusely for being late but once again I had been set up for failure and I had let her down. This affected my relationship with her as she was a very busy lady herself and her time was precious and I had let her down. Anthony's behaviour was that he had to come first and that my attention should be focused on him entirely.

On another occasion I had arranged to go to my friend's home for dinner. Anthony came in from work and said that he had tickets for an event for that evening. I was not aware of this but he accused me of knowing and forgetting about it. So yet again putting the blame on me and controlling me with his behaviour. I then had to get in touch with my friend who had prepared the dinner and obviously had to let her down. You may well say, why the heck did I let my friend down, for him. I was confused and he made me believe he had got the tickets a lot earlier. He made me doubt myself because of his ability to create confusion. What actually happened was that he knew I was going out for dinner in advance and had booked those tickets that very same day and came home and accused me of double booking saying I knew about them when I didn't. If I was to call him a liar or go against what he had said I would be made to feel stupid. Of course, I am trying to keep the peace in the house, so I went along with his wishes and demands to maintain an aura of peace in the home. I was partly my own worst enemy as I didn't stand up to him enough and this basically was my nature. A stronger woman would have dealt with him completely differently as did my good friend and neighbour Laney. He threatened to rip her head off her shoulders because he was intimidated by her as she was a really strong woman. He thought by threatening her, as she had told me numerous times to go to the police, she would be frightened of him. By the way he didn't do this himself he sent me round to her home with his message. But it had the exact opposite effect as she phoned the police herself but unfortunately they didn't act on what they had been told. When she was going out one day he was cleaning the car and she stopped her car outside, wound the window down, and told him to grow a pair of balls and if he wanted to threaten her with violence he now had the chance. He just ignored her and turned is his head away and didn't look back. She shouted to him that he was only good for beating weak women and couldn't handle someone strong. She told him he was a coward. She also said she hadn't finished with him. Again he was trying to destroy my friendship with Laney yet another one he tried to break up. However, he didn't succeed but she did move away and we lost contact but we are now writing this book together. She suggested to me to write my story because it may help me to cleanse and heal and if one person found help from reading my story then that is my gift to them.

There were many times socially when Anthony and I went out to parties and we both drank. There were times when we both drank too much but it didn't seem to have the same effect as we were having fun in our relationship. It was only in the latter part of our marriage that he didn't like me drinking as he was climbing the career ladder and I was a show wife and he thought it would ruin his reputation. He just really wanted a wife that sat there and said absolutely nothing. I have to laugh as I don't think he will ever find a woman like that. I can now openly admit that I did have a problem with alcohol during my marriage to Anthony and this was triggered by something he said or did before we went out or whilst we were out. I was always upset before we went out and he knew that I used to drink whilst in this state. He perpetuated the scenario to further control me. My weakness for drinking to drown out my pain and the abuse I was suffering helped him control me more and I sank to the very bottom of the tank really. I gradually became more and more depressed and was always at the doctors. My medical records show the pattern of my life and utilising alcohol made me even more depressed. An example is when we were invited for a weekend away to some friends in Rawtenstall. They were a nice genuine couple with three small children. These were friends of Anthony's as we never went out with friends of mine – I had none left. They were far enough away from our lives not to really know him very well. He was alarmingly charming and superficial with them. Now before we went up to their home, Anthony did something really upsetting to me, shouting abuse about something I had done or not done and getting very angry with me, screaming inches away from my face. This was terrifying and when we arrived I was very nervous and had a drink to drown it out. This then gave him the opportunity and ammunition to use against me whilst we were there in private or when we got home. He then persecuted me for at least a week. The fact that they were all drinking just as much if not more was irrelevant. I usually went to bed before them and left them downstairs drinking. The majority of times where I lost control he had triggered this effect in me deliberately. I didn't understand this at the time but I do now.

Anthony used to tell his friends and his own family that I was an unfit mother and I could not be left with my son overnight so he would ask these friends to look after him when he was on business overnight trips to make me look really bad. But on the other hand he went away on a week's holiday abroad with his daughter on a motorbike to Austria and left me with my son who was perfectly alright with me then. But when it was a business thing he used to get one of my son's friends parents to look after him for that one night to make sure that my son realised that I was an unfit mother. It was easy for my son to believe this as I had had periods where I had drunk to excess when Anthony had usually deliberately caused upset to me. I used drink to protect myself from what Anthony was doing to me. It was my crutch to help me from falling into the abyss, i.e. having a mental breakdown.

Towards the end of my marriage, we had a massive argument, about three weeks before we went to a wedding. It was on a Saturday morning and I was telling him that I would not be his victim anymore and he would not destroy me. My son had intervened as he was really upset and tried to stop the argument. I calmed down and we went ahead with our daily routine cleaning the house etc. Boring! That's what he liked to do not me but I had to do it and had no option otherwise there was trouble ahead. Usually it was my head. Three weeks later on the day of the wedding, the groom came to our house on the Saturday morning to get himself ready. After getting ready Anthony asked me if I would drive them both to a pub in Sale so they could have a drink prior to the wedding. I said that this gave me very little time to get ready as it was about an hour's round trip. However, I gave in and took them to the pub. When I got back home I had to rush so as not to be late for the wedding and I had told Anthony's daughter and my son Connor that I would be returning later to take them to the party after the wedding. At this point I was doing all the driving so obviously I had not had a drink. I then arrived at the wedding just in time and Anthony was stood outside the door shouting "Where have you been?" his face all twisted in anger. His mouth was wide open as he was shouting.

He was quite frightening and I'm sure if there hadn't been anyone else around he would have launched at me.

I was now late because of him changing the arrangements. We rushed into the wedding room and only just got in before the bride. I was in a state of panic how awful would that have been. My breathing was heavy and I was upset.

On another occasion I was invited to the Health Club, it was a lovely sunny day and a Saturday, Katherine and Matt Harding were sat outside in the sun when I arrived. I said to Katherine that I would not be staying that long as I was going to visit my mum. I had tried to phone my mum, as she was suffering from dementia, but received no reply. I was therefore very worried about her and her whereabouts. I thought she may have gone out with my brother John shopping so I decided to stay at the Health Club with them. Katherine went and got me a glass of wine and of course Anthony would not have liked this. She was sat with her partner so I didn't really suspect anything about the offer of a glass of wine. I remember Katherine going to the toilet which she often did when she wanted to use her phone, as I had caught her lots of times. I did not think any more about it though. Imagine the scene as I was sat at the table and my glass of wine was over the other side of the table as I had put it down in the shade and gone to sit in the sun. About fifteen minutes later Anthony appears and comes to talk to me outside. How did he know I was there as I was going to visit my Mum? I had called in at the Health Club because Katherine had phoned me and asked me to go. Why had she done that as she was with her partner? I believe it was to set me up on purpose. When Anthony came over to talk to me he made it clear that he was looking at the wine, so how did he know that was my glass of wine. He then went back into the club lounge area and sat with his friend Jack who was already there. They sat having a drink discussing the university that they both attended. He was a friend who played squash with Anthony and was from Liverpool. I at that point had finished my glass of wine and Katherine said to me that I shouldn't let him tell me what to do and I needed to stand up for myself. I became annoyed about it. She then went on to say would I like another glass of wine. I said "Yes" which was weak of me but when it came I didn't drink it. However, the private dick, namely Anthony had had his beady eyes on me watching every move I made. I had actually only had one glass of wine. I then went to speak to Anthony about us going out that evening for a late birthday meal for me. This must have been about late September time or early October and the weather was still lovely for that time of year. When I spoke with Anthony, in front of his friend, about the evening he couldn't have been nastier and blanked me completely. I then left the club very upset and went back home. He came in later that evening and we had yet another argument and I was frightened of him as usual. He was angry and vicious and I knew it would end up in yet another beating. I was so distressed that I spent the night on the street drinking a bottle of wine by myself. At this point I knew something was really wrong but was really so confused and I am still confused about some of the events. I then found myself outside somebody's house in Davyhulme in the early hours of the morning; the occupants took me into their home and were very concerned about me as I had stated I was too terrified to go home. They called the police and the policeman could not determine the full facts because of my confusion and alcohol. He felt I was unsafe to be taken home and maybe a vulnerable adult in society as I had stated to him that one minute my husband was wonderful and then the next he was a total bastard, Jekyll and Hyde personality. The policeman couldn't determine what I was talking about which was not surprising really because I couldn't either. I was then taken to my mums' house. Every time I ended up like this the perpetrator was always Katherine and she had set me up yet again.

The mental abuse began shortly after the honeymoon period of about three years and I now think I even married him knowing he had these underlying issues. However, I felt sorry for him with the history of abuse by his own father that he had told me about. The actual physical side of it started before my son Connor was born. I had had many periods of screaming and shouting at me as I thought his head would leave his shoulders with the ferocity of his rage. It also began on holiday with my daughter. We had gone to America with Laney and her hubby. We were staying in a villa at Kissimmee in Florida. He was very controlling with me but quite sadistic towards my daughter Rachel as Connor was only a baby. Anthony had started to pick Rachel up out of bed early in the morning and go and throw her in the pool whist still half asleep and in her nightie. I know this because Laney and Martin looked a bit disturbed by it all. Laney told me at a later stage what she had thought of Anthony and found his behaviour to be abusive to my daughter and quite sadistic and cruel. After throwing her into the pool, he would not let her do anything until she had done a lot of sums. He got quite angry if she got any wrong and her little face looked terrified. Not surprising really as his face was only inches away from hers. Laney was so upset and angry with him she and Martin went their separate ways in the second week of the holiday. She told me she found it more and more difficult to keep her thoughts to herself but did not wish to spoil the holiday for me and the children. So she left it at that.

On the Sunday after we returned from the holiday I was at work in intensive care and Rachel was wearing the yellow princess dress we had bought from the fun fair in Florida when I left home that morning. I received a phone call (by text on my bleep) and I rang my home number back. It was around lunchtime on the day and I spoke to Anthony who was in a very angry mood. He screamed to me that my daughter Rachel had done something he didn't like and he was very unhappy with her. I asked why he was calling me at work as I couldn't just leave to deal with it and she was only a little girl. She was about nine but was very small for her age and dainty. He appeared to be very distressed on the phone and I felt something had happened where I did needed to go home. I finished treating my patient and advised staff that I had to go home and would return later. It was only ten minutes to my house. I found Anthony extremely angry, ranting and raving, and Rachel was shaking with fear and really upset. I could not quite get to the facts as to what had happened at that point. I felt really uncomfortable leaving her there so I contacted my ex-husband, Rachel's dad, who only lived around the corner and made arrangements to take her to his house for the afternoon, which I did. I was so relieved as Rachel was a quiet child and rarely naughty. I think she was like this due to the terror that he reigned over her.

I then returned back to work and decided that I would sort the situation out when I got home that day. When I arrived home that evening Anthony had a story ready for me about what had happened in his opinion. He said he was bathing Connor who was about a year old and he had shouted Rachel to the bathroom and asked her to go and get some mousse. Rachel in her innocence brought back her toy moose which was a beany bag. Anthony was actually really requesting shampoo to wash Connor's hair and she had returned without the hair mousse. At which point, from what I could gather from Rachel, Anthony went ballistic picked Rachel up by her neck and carried her back into her bedroom, still holding her by her neck, which was just the next room to the bathroom. He had his hands firmly around her little throat whilst she was dangling in mid-air. He then threw her onto her bed fiercely and began to rant and rave at her whilst he had left Connor in the bath on his own. He went on to add that he had then made a decision to call me after finishing bathing Connor.

As I was not there, again it is difficult to prove, and recently Rachel told me exactly what had happened to her that day but will not speak out about it. I think she is still terrified of what he may do if he finds out. She also brought it up that he went into the bedroom and was smacking them at night – my children and his own. Again I did not know about this either. The only time that I saw him trying to hit Rachel I went and stood in front of him to prevent him from hitting her and told him not to touch a hair on her head and this was because she had been to a fireworks display and had come home and her boots were muddy and he nearly left the planet over that one. He didn't hit her as I remained in front of her.

The control from Anthony was also being extended to the children and definitely the abuse too. I do believe that if I hadn't been there he would have hit her and in his fury god knows what he would have done. I never agreed with him hitting the children so he did this behind my back whilst I was in bed telling them to be quiet or else. Quite nasty and vicious of him on top of the verbal abuse he was giving my daughter. There was always tension and fear in the air in our home, from the fear that arose from his controlling, bullying and abusive behaviour towards us all. We never ate a meal and swallowed properly as we always felt far too tense to eat and meal times were always extremely uncomfortable. I often said to him that I couldn't eat my food because I was so upset. It was like living with a Sergeant Major from the army. If Rachel scooped her food with a fork and her face was too close to the food he would shout at her, so loud she nearly jumped out of her seat, and make it known that that was not the way to eat? If her arms touched the table, i.e. elbows on the table he would go absolutely potty at her again shouting and frightening her so much she could hardly eat. I have learned from Rachel since the end of my marriage that she used to have a tissue on her lap and put some food in it because she was so nervous she couldn't swallow. When my son was born, I had to take Rachel to the doctors several times as she was not eating at home. I thought at the time that she may have been jealous of our new baby Connor. However, in hindsight I realised a lot of it was caused by the bullying behaviour of Anthony. We are very lucky that she didn't end up with an eating disorder. He tried to turn the children against me. He often used to say in front of the children that I was a really bad mother and often said that the food I had made for us all was just too disgusting to eat. She therefore felt like she couldn't eat it. He also told my friend Laney that I was a rubbish cook and my food was disgusting. I always had to have the dinner ready, often planning ahead the night before. I always had to look my best before having a meal and he fiercely insisted on this. He always wanted a warm welcome no matter what and he really needed this. He tried to get the children to prefer him and turn them against me. This made me feel mentally inadequate with his behaviour. He did all of this on purpose and he was very controlled and calculating and very often used to laugh and smile at me afterwards. I felt brave when drinking alcohol and only then did I try to challenge his behaviour but always ended up worst and then just drank more and more to sound out the screaming at me. I was also afraid to show any affection towards my children in case he took it out on them. I believed he was angry and tried to placate him, however, this was not really the case as he never got angry he was controlled with the shouting and abuse knowing exactly what he was doing and what he wanted to achieve which was total submission of us all. He was always completely in control of his emotions. These traits are often misunderstood by professional people but clearly show the actions and behaviours of a Sociopath. I tried to tell the police and social workers but was never believed as Anthony painted a perfect picture of himself as a really smart and super intelligent business man and me his wife the sad and helpless drunk. He also painted this picture of me to my son Connor constantly. He set me up all the time. He often would say to my friends and neighbours that I was an alcoholic even before I actually became one. I remember one particular time where he insisted I go to each neighbour in the cull-de-sac and tell them that I was an alcoholic. I was never to tell anyone that he was beating the living shit out of me on a regular basis though. Therefore, guess who they always believed. Yes true it wasn't me. He always used the word "only" as it minimised the effect of his actions. For example "it was only a slap" which he told the social worker about the attack in Greece. I have since obtained the evidence and had it translated and I wasn't lying but she believed him. Throughout, the abusive years I felt I was in the middle of a very confusing mess and that it must somehow be my fault. As Anthony always blamed me for everything, the children's behaviour, my behaviour, and even his own. He always used the children to try to control me. The word used is "CFC" cooking, fucking and cleaning. Also the word "WIFE" which was washing, ironing, fucking, etc. A lot of abusers often use these words to describe their wives and partners.

Some of the violence and physical attacks against me were in 2001 and were witnessed by Laney on two occasions. Laney has written a witness statement about these two incidents. One was where he had me by the throat and the other was where he had me pinned to the floor punching me in the head.

One particular weekend his abuse had got completely out of hand. He was screaming at me continuously getting within inches of my face and this was when Connor was about two years of age. Rachel would have been about ten years old. This screaming at me had been going on for months and months whilst I was going to work and trying to bring up the children. I was in the kitchen at the time washing up the dishes and he had a massive verbal attack. I had no idea where it came from it was like a volcano erupting out of the blue. I had not been drinking at all and was doing nothing wrong just simply washing up. I turned around to face him when he was screaming at me from behind and told him that I had had enough and I could not take any more of his abuse. I backed up to the kitchen cupboards and he still continued shouting and screaming in my face with his abuse. I was terrified and only the thoughts of escaping went through my mind. I had to get away from him. He then threatened to kill me if I ever left whilst grabbing me and shaking me. He did not hit me at that point. I went upstairs and got changed and went out without giving him a chance to start again. I went to an Italian Restaurant with work colleagues and it was near Christmas, I told everyone there that I had a horrible evening at home with Anthony. When I arrived home that evening I packed clothes for Rachel, Connor and myself to leave for a while. I wasn't sure what I was going to do I just knew I had to get away from him. I couldn't stand him near me anymore.

I plucked up the courage and told my friend Anne about this a few weeks later. It was a Saturday morning, early on; I got the children up out of bed whilst Anthony was downstairs in the front room drunk as he had been drinking all night on his own. I then left the house with the children. He was in his dressing gown sat in the chair and I said to him that we were leaving for a few days and he said nothing and didn't try to stop us. We went to my mum's house and stayed Saturday and Sunday. I had to go to work on Monday and the children had to go to school so I telephoned Anthony to say that I would not come home unless he had calmed down or at least could I get some clothes for us all for the Monday. He was calm on the phone and asked me to come home at which point I said that I would not tolerate any more of his behaviour. I returned home on the Sunday afternoon and he took me out to get a Christmas tree as if nothing had happened. After each abusive episode he always acted later as if nothing had happened. I bumped into Anne my friend and just said hello to her. I spoke to her the following week when she called round to my home and I actually started to tell her what had happened and the abuse that was going on in my life at the time. She said that I needed to get out of the marriage. She loved to gossip but she never said anything about what was going on in her life it was always about other's lives. She also told her twin sister Katherine all about it.

My mum bought me a book about how to understand men. I often used to be reading this self-help book when Katherine would turn up at my home, always uninvited. We would often read parts of the book together so she was well aware about my abusive marriage to Anthony. She actually knew everything that happened to me and appeared to be sympathetic at times.

# CHAPTER 4

# Anthony's Secret Life and Affairs

Anthony's behaviour, since my short departure to my mum's, improved for several years; although he was still very nasty, he screamed less. I believe he was having an affair with his secretary when the behaviour was at its worst. It detracts from what he was actually doing. Connor would have been about two or three years old at the time. I remember at the time speaking to my neighbour Laney, who was a business woman but also a Medium, she said by providing evidence to me of where she lived, what she looked like, her perfume and where they would be meeting must mean something. He even had his password for his computer as her last name. He explained this to me by saying it meant need some money for the bank details. How stupid did he think I was? Also he brought a card home from work after Christmas which had Superstar on the front of the card. Inside it was addressed to Anthony and was signed "with love from Kat xxx" which was his secretary. This card came home with him with other cards from work, however, he threw all the others away but kept hers hidden in his office at the very bottom of a pile of papers. *He always threw mine and my children's cards away so why did he keep that one?* I asked myself. The words which Laney had told me echoed through my mind.

I never told him that I had found the card but I did tell Katherine my friend that I had found it. I remarked to her that I was sure he was having an affair. I also told her what my friend Laney had told me about him and the evidence that was given by her communicators. When he knew many years later that I was petitioning for divorce I looked and the card was still in its hiding place. When I went to get the card three weeks later, and just before I was leaving, the card had been removed.

I actually remember seven major attacks against myself because they were so very bad and painful that I couldn't possibly forget them but I know there were many more. I believe I have blotted a lot out over the years as I couldn't face it all. The next major attack came when it was his 40th birthday present. I had arranged for a holiday to Greece in a 4★ hotel for his 40th. There was only myself, Anthony and Connor going on the holiday. This is now about ten years ago and Connor would have been around eight at the time. I had worked a lot of overtime at work to enable me to give Anthony this surprise holiday as I was still trying to make my marriage work at the time. I know you must think I'm mad. We were flying on the 17th August 2006 which happened to be 'A' Level results day for Rachel. I had not realised this at the time of booking. When I realised I told Rachel I would contact her on the day from Greece to find out her results. She hadn't wanted to come on the holiday with us; not surprising from the previous abuse she had suffered at the hands of her step dad Anthony. It was quite an event on this particular day when we arrived at the airport and one of the bags was slightly overweight and he blamed me. So the start was not good. We only had to adjust the weight by transferring some of the contents into the other bag to balance them out. However, this resulted in him being in a foul mood. We had a four hour flight in front of us so not a good start to the holiday and I felt really uncomfortable. I did stupidly think he may get better when we got there as I had arranged a chauffeur driven taxi just for us to get to the hotel, which he really liked and was overly impressed with this, he thought he was important as he was getting something special. He always liked to feel important. When we arrived at the beautiful hotel we initially went to the coffee room as it was all inclusive. I had a coffee, he had a beer and Connor a coke. Anthony then said after our drinks he would take Connor to the room to unpack their cases. I said that I would just remain there a little longer and ordered myself a half of lager. I always drank when I was upset and he hardly spoke to me at all during the flight. I then went up to the room and started unpacking my case. He didn't seem to notice that I had had a drink. We all had a rest and then got ready for dinner in the restaurant. We went to dinner and had a lovely meal and enjoyed ourselves with a glass of wine each. We may have even had two glasses of wine as, we weren't driving, and we were on holiday. We then all went and sat in the side lounge near the reception area. We started to play card games with Connor but it was a very controlled time by Anthony. I realised that I hadn't rung Rachel to find out about her 'A' Level results. I did have my mobile with me but it wasn't a very good one, resembled an old brick, but I took it off to the loos to make a phone call to Rachel. I couldn't get through to her. I knew Anthony had a really good mobile but because I know he did not like Rachel I was reluctant to ask him for the use of his phone to call her. He wouldn't have liked the fact that I wanted to call her on holiday. I felt the mood and tension in him knowing him really well and it was only to be likened to a volcano waiting to erupt. I therefore toddled off to reception telling Anthony I was going to the loo again. I asked reception for the area code for the UK and he told me there was a phone in the bedroom so I had the area code and went to the room to make my call. Yet again I could not get through to Rachel so I went back to sit with him and Connor. At this point we both had another glass of wine as it was all-inclusive. I was trying to work out how, in my head, I was ever going to be able to contact my daughter as this was a very important day for her. I gave a reasonable length of time before going back to reception and asking was the code they gave me correct. He said that I needed to insert a '0' before the number he had given me. I went back to the room and the correct codes and finally reached her. I was becoming quite anxious now. She had done really well getting the grades she required to get into university and I was so elated for her. I quickly returned to Anthony so as not to let him know I had made the call to Rachel. I could tell at this point, even though he didn't know what I was doing, he looked in a foul mood. I said to Anthony that I was tired and could we all go to bed. He agreed with me and we went back to the room. Anthony was still drinking in the room and was sat on the balcony, Connor had gone to bed which was in the room with us. I went and sat with Anthony on the balcony and we had a row, I actually confronted him during the row telling him what I had done, shamelessly calling my own daughter to ascertain her exam results. I then told him that I thought there was something seriously wrong with him and he needed some help as he was always in a foul mood. Even on a lovely holiday it didn't make a difference to his mood. Eventually as I was getting nowhere with him and fed up with the arguing I decided to go to bed. I presume he continued to drink all night on the balcony as he didn't come to bed. I lay awake for a considerable amount of time, could have been one hour or even two as I could not get to sleep. I felt so tense I decided to get up and my intention was to go for a walk to help calm me down to sleep. I had reached the door and opened it but the next minute Anthony came like a bat out of hell from the balcony, grabbed me and threw me to the floor. He then positioned himself on top of me holding my arms down with his knees. He put one of his hands around my throat and then he punched and punched me in the face so many times with the other one until the people next door to our room had heard the noise as I was screaming with pain and fear and alerted the management. I thought that he was going to kill me. The residents of the next room telephoned reception to advise what they were hearing and the man from the reception came up into our room as I had not had time to shut the door before Anthony pounced on me. The man came into the room and shouted to Anthony to "Get off her and stop hitting her". Remember my son was in the room at the same time in his bed. I had managed to knee him in the balls and get one of my arms free and rip his watch off. At this point, knowing someone else was there watching him and witnessing this, he got off me and the Greek police were called by the hotel. They took Anthony away with them around 3am. Then the police and the hotel staff took me to a room and asked what I wanted to do about it. I was too scared to say anything at all as I was by now terrified for my life and that one day he may very well kill me. I thought if I did anything against him he would take it out on me and the children. The police wanted to lock him up and I think he may have spent the night in the cells but can't remember as I was too severely traumatised by the whole event. The police wanted me to pursue this and take action against Anthony but I was too terrified. Later that day he arrived back at the hotel and we went back to the room at which point we had yet another disagreement and he blamed it all on me saying it was all my fault. I got up stating that I was going to get my passport and go back home and leave him there. I wanted to take Connor with me and did not want to leave him there with Anthony. He then changed his tactics by saying he was sorry and basically reminded me that we were on a two week holiday and let's try to enjoy ourselves. I do remember though the next day Connor asking me several times why I had marks around my neck.

Further into the holiday when we were both sunbathing Anthony came and sat by my chair as he thought I may pursue divorce on my arrival back in the UK. He did a lot of what I call creeping around me for the next few days trying to get things back on track by reminding me what we had together. Being the fool that I was I tried to believe him. A few days later we went out for the day using a taxi with a lady taxi driver. He never stopped going on about how beautiful she was in front of me. We were then walking down the street towards the shops and came across a high spec jewellers. He told me that for his 40th I was buying him a big thick gold bracelet which cost £800. I thought at the time that he was completely mad and I jokingly said well I'll have a treat too then. I got the feeling that he didn't want me to have a treat. However, I bought myself a small gold ring. He was not at all pleased. I remember thinking there is something definitely wrong with this man but what do I do about it. I was quite scared about being on my own again with Connor as I had been through this with my previous marriage. I would like to add that at the divorce proceedings Anthony had the Greek event removed from the petition saying that it never happened. I had it put back in having gone to all of the travel agents in my area and finding the date and hotel name of our holiday and I telephoned the hotel. I spoke to a member of staff advising what I needed from them, evidence or a record of the attack on me, with regard to our holiday and the beating I had taken. The member of staff I spoke to, not sure if he was the manager or not, but he said he would look into it as he didn't like men who hit women. He asked me to ring back about six weeks later. It was actually three months before I managed to speak to that man again. To my absolute astonishment he had only found the record of that night's event in the hotel log written of course in Greek. He read it out to me in English which explained the whole event. The description was exactly as I remember that evening's events and I asked for it to be faxed through and I asked for it to be in Greek as that would show that I hadn't made it up and it was genuine as I would have to get it translated into English. I was very lucky as my sponsor at the time had a daughter who had been married to a Greek and she translated it for me. It was then entered into the divorce petition as evidence to support my version of the truth. He couldn't say it hadn't happened now as there were witnesses to the incident.

Some years and many moods later my daughter arrived for a visit with her boyfriend. She lived with us at the time and was in her third year of university. The first year she spent at home, the second she lived in university residence and the third year she came home as she could no longer afford to be paying the rent even with my contributions. She had met Nige and was in a steady relationship with him in her third year of university. Nige had no job at this point in time. Rachel came in to the kitchen with Nige and said we have something to tell you. I had been at work all day and was still in my uniform. Rachel then went onto say that she was pregnant. I was, to be fair, not overjoyed to start off with as she had not finished her university course. Nige had no job and I was also concerned that we were all going on a holiday for my 50th birthday present to Australia and she was going to be on a 24hr plane flight. It was not very good timing for anybody really so I was not that happy to be honest. I also knew that Anthony would go mental about it as I knew him very well and it would be another reason for him to continue with his abuse against me. I did find out at a later date that Nige and Rachel had decided that they wanted a family so it was a deliberate act to get pregnant which surprised me at the time as he was supposed to be a devout Christian and Rachel was a born again Christian. They had nowhere to live together and no money behind them. I immediately, being a rescuer, started to try and plan what we could do to help them. They then left, saying and feeling that I wasn't going to congratulate them on their surprise, but I couldn't at that point as I had too many worries about them and how Anthony was going to react when they had gone. They actually came at 4.30pm on a Monday evening and I had an awful feeling about the situation for them and how I was going to tell Anthony. I had already felt some weeks earlier that someone around me was pregnant. I had told Anthony at that time what I felt and that I felt it was me. Stupid really as I had been sterilised. His reaction was that it didn't matter anyway as I would just have to go and get an abortion. I then did not discuss this with him any further leaving the conversation as it was. There was no point as I couldn't get through to him.

This had all come about two to three weeks before we were going on a holiday of a lifetime to Australia which cost about £11,000. I felt that when Rachel and Nige had told me about the pregnancy and that it was an accident I had thought to myself later, well ok, we will all just have to deal with it and help them the best we could. However, that was not to be and I hadn't yet told Anthony about this as I didn't or couldn't summon up the courage. It took me several hours to pluck up the courage to broach the subject with him. I got him upstairs out of my son's way so we were in the bedroom at the time, I have vague memories of what actually happened, it was like an explosion and was really ugly. I could only liken it to mount Vesuvius erupting. There was no way to reason with Anthony in a logical way. I could understand him being upset as Rachel was in the last year of her degree and we had supported her with food and finances. You would expect to talk about it in a reasonable manner but that was not the case as Anthony had very fixed views and kept saying to me that he was a man of principle and he was going to throw her out of the house. As usual I tried to placate him and pleaded with him not to be so rash and hasty with his decision as I knew we were all going on holiday together in two weeks. I knew how bad it would be on the holiday and asked Anthony if we could talk about it after the holiday. He flatly refused and yet again I got the blame me for it all. Laughable now, but not then. He then told me that if he had been allowed to do all the parenting of Rachel this would never have happened and it was completely my fault as to why this had happened. Don't know why I expected a different outcome to the problem as I was always to blame for everything that happened in his life and our life together, even if I hadn't had anything to do with it. So you can understand when I tell you it was an especially unhappy time for me knowing that my husband was about to throw my daughter out of our house as I have mentioned it was the last year of her degree, Nige was unemployed and therefore they would have no money and nowhere to stay.

I later found out some months after our holiday that their pregnancy was a deliberate act and had been planned all along. So I was not happy with this revelation they made. In some respects this impacted upon my relationship or whatever relationship I had left with Anthony. He was going mental with me on the one side, I was trying to protect my daughter and she was going mental with me on the other side by saying what am I going to do and where are we going to live. You would have thought in their planning that they would have broached this. Anthony went as far as to say that he thought I was a bad mother. I have read since the breakup and my recovery from alcohol that this is a tactic that a sociopath uses to undermine you all the time.

I will now describe the events from this point forward to the end of our holiday. It was my worst nightmare and believe it or not was supposed to be my 50th birthday present from the person who I was married to. A memory and event that the majority of us would love to treasure and look back on with love and laughter. I would really like to call him a Psycho really as he was a f...g nutter. Funnily enough, I ended up looking like one at the end and thank god I got out. Back to the holiday. Anthony's brother Doogle married an Australian who was working in the UK at the time. They married in Australia and we went to the wedding. It was a really lovely occasion we met her father and his wife. Her father had paid for the wedding and it was very expensive affair. We had stayed with them for the wedding and we all got on really well. When they offered us a week's holiday in Australia in Brisbane we thought it was a great idea. We found ourselves a hotel for the first week of our holiday in Sydney. So we thought that everything was organised and were happy with it all. We had paid for the flights from Sydney to Brisbane to coincide with the second week to stay at their house. We received an email from them to say her brother and family from the UK were going to stay with them at the same time we had been invited so we couldn't stay with them after all. However, they did find us a holiday home for the second week which of course cost us £700 for the week for all five of us. The costs were now escalating and then Rachel told me that she didn't really want to go now because she knew that she had a lot of work to do for her degree. I thought to myself I can't believe this as Rachel had already asked for Anthony's own daughter Charlene to come with us for company for her. We had already shelled out for this too. I explained to Rachel that we couldn't get our money back as it was weeks before we were flying out and that she could do her work whilst we were out there and we could accommodate that in our plans. She moaned somewhat and said she was pregnant and may not be feeling very well and it was a long flight. I told her there was nothing we could do at this stage of the plans as it was too late so she would have to come with us. I also discussed with her at this time the fact she had said that her and Nige may be able to go and live with his Dad in his spare room. She wasn't too happy with this as she was not happy with his cleanliness as she was very particular about being clean and she felt it would not be appropriate for a baby. I said if the worst came to the worst I would have to ask my mum and dad if they could stay there. Nige's mum still had four other children living with them so she couldn't accommodate any more people living in her home.

Just days before going to Australia I contacted my local Citizens Advice Centre and they advised me to come into the centre and they would give me a slot on the Monday morning. Subsequently, I went and sat there waiting for about an hour and a half. I desperately needed to know information about what my daughter Rachel could get help with and if there were any type of benefit that she could be entitled to and what timescale through her pregnancy it might be at. I never got to see anybody as I had to leave and go to my mum and dad's house because I wanted to speak to my dad in person about borrowing some money from him to help Rachel and Nige set up a home together. I did speak with the advisor on the desk at the centre telling her I couldn't wait any longer and explained the situation to her. She advised me that Rachel would be entitled to some benefits but not until six months into her pregnancy. At that point I knew that the rent that needed to be found would be at least four months' worth of rent before they were entitled to any benefits. I then went to see my dad, who was eighty six years old, to advise about the situation and to see if he could help financially to pay for the rent of a flat for Rachel and Nige. Dad wasn't totally happy with the situation and said he would speak to Anthony to say that when you take the responsibility of a child on that you must see it through to the end. My dad was the most honest person I have ever known and a real gentleman. He, being the marvellous dad that I had known throughout my life agreed to lend me the money although he thought that it was Anthony's responsibility to help them. I felt so relieved when I left my mum and dad's house but also angry that I had been put in this situation by Anthony wanting to throw her out. Before going away on holiday I spoke with Rachel and advised her on what I had done. She told me that she had spoken to her previous employer who had a flat on top of the hairdressers that she owned and that they could possibly go there. She would also let them have the flat at a much cheaper rental price than I could have found anywhere else. Rachel's previous employer was a really lovely lady so I was relieved at hearing this. It had lessened some of my anxiety about the whole situation. We said to each other that we would sort it all out after our holiday.

This was all done behind Anthony's back as I knew he would forbid me to offer any help to my own daughter and he would go mental with me again. I was terrified of Anthony and always did my very best to keep the peace. Anthony had also refused to speak to my dad when he had telephoned the house to speak with Anthony. He would not speak to my dad and never did. I felt that I was piggy in the middle with Rachel needing my help as a mum and trying to be a wife to a dominant controlling narcissistic sociopath. My fear of him rendered me incapable of facing up to him without a drink.

When arriving at the airport for our long awaited holiday of a lifetime, I felt like I had hit a brick wall when Anthony's daughter Charlene who I mentioned earlier asked me a big favour. Wait for it, she only asked me to speak to her dad and tell him that she smoked like a chimney and drank like a fish and her dad didn't know. God I thought what the hell next. I didn't tell him before the flight as I didn't want a volcanic eruption on the way to Oz. I braved it a few days into the holiday and he had actually seen her having a drink, she was only twenty years old, which was her choice but I always I ended up piggy in the middle and in front of the firing squad. Also whilst at the airport Rachel had wanted something to eat, which isn't uncommon when you are pregnant, so we went along to one of the shops and were looking for a healthy option to eat. She then stated at that time when I was looking for food for her, that she wanted lots of children with Nige, before I nearly died and went to heaven she mentioned the figure ten. I thought good god they have nowhere to live no money and now they are having ten children. I can laugh now but it wasn't funny at the time. We eventually got on the flight with all the drama behind me, or so I thought. During the flight we were all served with our meals as they do, however, Rachel didn't like anything that was on offer except some of the fruit. I had aportion of fruit for desert so I offered her my fruit as well. Anthony was incredibly nasty to me about what I had done and told me to stop feeding that animal. I was absolutely disgusted and horrified at his attitude. I was also worried in case anyone seated in front or behind us had heard him. Although it was a difficult situation and not what we would have envisaged for Rachel it was however something we had to deal with as adults. When I eventually reached Oz I was at my wit's end with it all. I was actually starting my holiday of a lifetime feeling quite depressed and feeling physically sick and was not at all looking forward to the two weeks. During the holiday Anthony completely ignored Rachel but made a strong emphasis on continually hugging his daughter Charlene and being affectionate towards her. Charlene spoke with me in the second half of the holiday asking me could I tell Anthony to stop hugging her as that was not how her family had treated her and she didn't like it. Again I was used as the tool to deliver the message to him and his reaction was as expected and stating that he was trying to be a good dad now after ignoring his children for the previous years of their life. He threw a wobbler and went into the bedroom and stayed there for hours on the bed. He actually threw his toys out of the pram and spat his dummy out. I went in to try to talk to him but he wouldn't listen to me. I thought to myself at the time that he had been drinking and actually he was a very heavy drinker.

Upon arrival in Oz I telephoned my mum and dad as I still needed to reassure myself that I could borrow that money as the situation was going deeper and deeper into a black hole. My mum and dad were so supportive and I said that I would pay them back when I could. For the first week we stayed in a hotel in Sydney with great rooms, Rachel and Charlene in one room, Anthony myself and Connor in another. He was about twelve at the time but it was cheaper for us to do it this way. Rachel was off her food and could not eat breakfasts and by the second or third morning Rachel did not even want to join us for breakfast downstairs. I was sat downstairs for breakfast with Anthony and Connor and he was becoming really very angry as he felt he had paid for the quite expensive breakfasts. He said to me that if she did not get herself down to have breakfast with us he was going to send her back to the UK on a plane on her own. He wouldn't have done this as he was too tight and he would have had to pay for the flight. Then because of all the drama about it I couldn't eat my breakfast as I felt so sick. I then took myself upstairs to their room and asked Rachel to come down and just join us if nothing else. I remember feeling really down and depressed with an overwhelming feeling that this was going to be a shit holiday. I told her what he had said and I felt torn between the two of them. She did eventually come down and pretended to have something. She then returned to her room to do her work for her degree. However, this required an internet connection for her computer so I asked for this to be added to our bill at the end of the week. He found out about this when he received the bill and he demanded this money back from Rachel. In fact he demanded it back many times. Rachel did join us one day and we went to a café bar for lunch but she only wanted some bread. So I got up and went to get some bread for her. Upon returning he was angry and upset. He showed me nothing but total contempt towards me for helping my daughter. I really did feel so sick now it took me all my time not to throw up. I would have just loved the earth to open up and swallow me. My life on holiday was pure hell he made it so awful that I was unable to relax and I wasn't allowed to enjoy myself because I wasn't doing what he wanted.

There were many other events, but during the second week of our holidays we went out for a meal, just Anthony and myself. After our lunch we went for a walk and window shopping. Feeling the atmosphere was maybe slightly more relaxed and we were on our own together I tried to speak to him about the Rachel situation. Basically, he went absolutely mental with me and went into a terrific rage so much so I thought his head would leave his shoulders, but in reality I was terrified. Everyone in the vicinity must have seen and heard this violent eruption. There was no talking to that man or reasoning with him in any shape or form. That evening we were at his brother Doogle's in laws for a meal. I had spoken to the wife about the situation and that I was upset and that he didn't like me to drink and that he was throwing my daughter out. She told me that a similar situation had happened with her daughter getting pregnant and she was actually gay so had no intention of staying with the man. She went on to have her baby and together with her female partner they were bringing the child up, which was about three at the time. She stated to me that her husband wasn't over the moon about it but was very supportive and just got on with it. She found it really strange that Anthony was being so difficult about it all. I had started to have a drink that evening as I felt so tense and upset about the whole thing. That evening the wife brought me over a drink to cheer me up she said but I thought god this is strong. I wouldn't normally put that amount of alcohol in my drinks and having already had a couple prior to this I completely lost it and told him what I thought of him in front of everyone and his daughter Charlene. Again, no one had seen his behaviour earlier on in the day so of course he blamed it all on me as he always did. He was totally unable to take any kind of responsibility for his actions and the consequences from them. The only way that I could ever confront Anthony about anything was when I had had enough alcohol to make me feel brave enough to do it. So you can imagine how embarrassing it was for me and the morning after he made me go downstairs and apologise for my behaviour. I was often instructed to do these types of things by him. He would set me up for a big fall. If I didn't follow his orders I would only incur yet another beating. Sounds pathetic really but it was easier for me to just give in to avoid the consequences.

We stayed for two days with the in-laws – Christmas Day and Boxing Day and then we moved on the following day to the apartment in Brisbane for the last week of our holidays. On Christmas Day at their home they were catering for a large number of people, probably about twenty if my memory serves me correctly. She had cooked the turkey and all the trimmings but then told me on the day that Anthony and I were expected to do all the clearing up after the meal. I thought this was really strange as I would have helped anyway and we were guests in their home. Everyone on Christmas Day had had a lot to drink and all were very merry and enjoying themselves as you would. I was left to do all the tidying up with her husband not mine he sat and did nothing. The next morning I went downstairs and said I would like to help with anything she needed to be done. She gave me a duster and asked me to clean the lounge and sweep round, which I was quite happy to do. But then she asked me to clean the toilets which I wasn't quite as happy to do. I would never have asked a guest of mine to do the toilets. However, I did clean the downstairs toilet and no more.

Boxing Day was Rachel's 21st birthday and I had bought a card and a couple of small gifts which I gave to her and wished her a really happy birthday. She was sat reading a book at the time. She thanked me for the presents. Anthony never said a word or wished her anything and I would say that the air was like ice and I remember thinking to myself at the time you miserable bastard and I wished that he was dead for what he had done to us all. Thank God we moved the next day.

During the second week we visited Doogle and his wife for lunch and they had two massive dogs and it was filthy in their home. I sat outside and I actually had to go in and get something to clean the table with as my arms were sticking to it. Yuk it was horrible. When we were sitting outside, Doogle and his wife had the audacity to tell us that their in laws who we stayed with were less than happy with us. I asked why the hell not. Doogle said that we had not tidied up after ourselves. I sat there gobsmacked as they had been less than hospitable to us and I had cleaned for them. It was a miserable holiday and later on that evening again I turned to alcohol to relieve my depression and anxiety. I heard them all leave and Anthony took the children back to the holiday home. He came into the room where I was sleeping, or so he thought, I was actually awake but I didn't want to go back with them. He then left. At that point in the holiday and my life

I thought of going out into the forest area around their home and just dying. I felt exhausted and drained by everything, the tension and the behaviour from Anthony was getting too much for me. The next day Doogle took me back to the holiday home to join them. We went out and about but it was so hard to enjoy myself with the negative air around us. Connor was just dragged around everywhere with no-one taking any notice of him and my heart went out to him. I just wanted to get home and I was right to want this as it didn't get any better.

On New Year's Eve the in laws were having a party and we had bought a lot of alcoholic drinks for this party as we knew that Doogle didn't have a lot of money. The daft thing is that we didn't get there. I actually refused to go as I did not want to be around all that alcohol. The girls went to the party and Anthony stayed with me and Connor. I mentioned to Anthony my concerns about them being able to get back to us that evening as they had no money. He relented and gave them the taxi fare. Rachel told me the next day that the wife had been most unpleasant to her at the party and she hadn't understood why. I was relieved that I hadn't gone we just sat and watched TV that evening. I remember looking at Connor that evening and he seemed very quiet and drained. He was a twelve year old boy absorbing all the negative energies around him constantly throughout the whole holiday. I was also concerned that Connor may learn this type of behaviour and end up like this himself. That evening Connor went to bed around ten. It was an open plan apartment and Connor's bed was just off the lounge area. We sat together on the sofa and Anthony approached me for sex. I said quietly that Connor was only just around the corner and he could get up at any minute and walk out and see us. I didn't feel it was appropriate at this time so I went to bed early on my own and did not see the New Year in. I remember lying in bed feeling really down and depressed and not knowing what I could do about the whole situation. I just knew it was not going to work out. Everyone was miserable and ungrateful and I was fed up of being around it all I had wanted was a lovely holiday and perhaps my expectations were too high. Was it too much too expect for me to have a lovely time for my 50$^{th}$ birthday. I'll never forget that birthday but for the wrong reasons words can't say just how bad it was.

I was so relieved to get home but there was yet another mountain for me to climb in the midst. When we arrived back the snow was thick and deep. We immediately put on the central heating and sat huddled around the fire. The girls said they were hungry and Charlene only ever ate chunky chicken with rice inherited from her mother. No sooner than Rachel had eaten, she said she was going to see Nige but as you can imagine her car was completely snowed in and I knew she wouldn't be able to drive off. I asked Anthony if he would help her to get her car out and for the first time he did as I think he just wanted to get rid of her. She could not have got away faster than she did and actually that was when she really left as she never came back, choosing to live at Nige's Dads. This however would not be appropriate for the baby. Charlene didn't stay either so I was left with Anthony, Mr Miserable Bastard. After she left all I heard coming from his miserable lips was that he wanted his thirty pounds back for the internet costs in the hotel. I would have loved to have got the thirty pounds and pushed it down his throat so he choked on it. That was only dreaming though. I then spoke again with my mum and dad and set her up in the flat above the hairdressers in Urmston. I used to go to visit taking them little parcels of food, tissues, loo roll etc. to help them as they had little money.

I was very lucky on this holiday as Anthony didn't hit me at all. He was vile and mentally abusive to me trying to undermine me in front of people but he didn't have the opportunity with everyone around us to beat me up. For that I was truly grateful.

Time moved on and Rachel and Nige decided to get married, I mean after all, he was a devout Christian and she was a born again Christian and the church they belonged to were frowning upon their behaviour. The church did not wish them to attend living in their circumstances. So Rachel and Nige began planning their wedding to placate the pastor of the church. Of course, again they had no money, and I was asked to help.

At this point I owed my dear mum and dad about £2,500 and now I had to try and find more money for a wedding. I asked if any other people could help them like her natural dad or Nige's parents and why were they coming to me. In the end I did want her to be happy and felt it was the right thing for them to marry. I bought her a wedding dress from a very upmarket expensive shop and paid a lot towards the wedding, i.e. cake and the registry office. Rachel's natural Dad paid half the fee for the registry office and I paid the rest. I paid for her shoes, her hairdresser's bill, I had to keep it all fairly low key as I had to carry out all the tasks behind Anthony's back. It was also very difficult as I couldn't access the bank account with my money in it as Anthony would have noticed the withdrawals from the joint account. I used my store credit card to purchase as much as I could as that was in my name only. It was the only way that it could be done to avoid him finding out.

I also paid for some of the meals for the reception. It wasn't a massive amount but it was all I had. It all had to be done really discreetly as I have just mentioned but also he had forbidden me to speak to her or for them to come to our home. He wouldn't even let her in the house. Anthony found out because his daughter Charlene was the bridesmaid but he didn't know I had helped. He told me that I was not allowed to go to the wedding of my own daughter but I stood up to him on this occasion and said that I was going to my own daughter's wedding. He was really angry with me but then shocked me the night prior to the wedding by saying to me that I could go and he would come with me. I told him he was not invited and Rachel did not want him there. The morning when I was getting ready to go with his daughter Charlene to the wedding he stood in front of me barring my exit from the room and saying right into my face that he wanted her keys back and the thirty pounds that she still owed him. I couldn't believe it and was laughing inside as his behaviour was so bizarre. I just left the house and really enjoyed the wedding and the day and we all had such a lovely time without him being there. I went home at the end of the day and he didn't speak to me as I had disobeyed him. As the weeks went by he would not allow me to put any pictures of my daughter's wedding up on the walls of our home. At home he was a different person than the personality he showed to those outside the home. He was like Dr Jekyll and Mr Hyde. I started to become more and more depressed and low for most of the time. He was often out playing squash, studying for his Master's degree or on his Harley Davison motorbike which cost £18,000 and I was not consulted about the cost. He just went out one day and bought it and then came home and let me know what he had bought. This wasn't the first motorbike he had bought as he had bought a Sportster Harley which was about £11K which he had traded in for the new bike. He treated the Harley like a God it was more important than any human in his life. I remember the first bike arriving the day prior to my being told on a Friday night that my dad may have only hours to live. I therefore had to rush over to a Stockport Hospital to see my dad. I rang Anthony in a bit of a state asking who could look after Connor. He was not compassionate at all he was driving home and told me I would just have to sort something out. A friend of a friend kindly offered after me making many phone calls. I then rushed over to the hospital. Thankfully he didn't actually pass over at that time he lived a further two years after that although my dad was still in hospital very poorly the next day. The motorbike arrived, the Sportster, and he was over the moon and got all his gear on and his mate who already had a bike arrived. He could not stop going on about his motorbike and I was incredulous as my dad was supposedly dying as per the hospital. I was totally beside myself with grief and any normal person would have spent some time with their wife. He went out with his mate on the motorbikes for the whole day. He spent thousands of pounds of motorbike gear for himself. That evening when he came home he never even asked how my dad was he just went on about how f...g great his motorbike was. I went to see my dad again in hospital and he came through his illness and was allowed home. I felt like I was living with a lodger in my home who played mind games with

69

me all the time. Rachel never came to visit as she knew that he hated her so I visited her when I could. I felt trapped in a spider's web and had no way to get out. Rachel then told me she was having twins and I remember thinking god how will she manage. Rachel achieved her degree to my great delight with a 2:1 two weeks before the twins were born. Anthony never ever saw the twins in hospital, my friend Anne came with me to see them. The twins were both boys and I was forbidden to visit them or for me to have any pictures up in the house of Rachel, Nige or the boys. He isolated me even from my own daughter. I tried on many occasions for him to relent and let them come in the house as Rachel was often crying down the phone to me asking why she could not visit me with her children. She did say to me that it was our house first mum. I told her that I was trying to get access but it was very difficult for me because he now had complete control over me, even though he was not in the house most of the time, often out on his motorbike, studying, playing squash, seeing his mates, and other women. I was very lonely and drank usually after him upsetting me in some way or other. This was usually before work or if I was ever going out deliberately trying to sabotage my day or evening. I actually believe that he planned most of it to ensure that I was really upset when I went to work or to the health club. He knew what triggered my drinking and he went overboard with his abuse. I used to try to call him to see what time he was coming in for his tea as I was terrified of it being late for him as he would really kick off. His phone was either off or he wouldn't even answer and I started to be scared to even ring him and I was totally isolated. Friends would only come over to see me if he wasn't there. They often said they were scared of him as once he threatened to rip my friend Laney's head off. On one occasion Rachel phoned the house to see if I had any oil she could use for her car as when she left she didn't take anything with her. Anne was in the house at the time and Anthony was there and I asked him about the oil and he went off on one not realising that Anne was in the kitchen. She overheard the shouting, screaming and aggression and she told me she was bloody terrified just to hear the way in which he spoke. I eventually found the oil and took it to my daughter to help her without him knowing as he would not have allowed me to give it to her. Little by little he was controlling my life removing people from it one by one with the exception of Anne's twin sister Katherine. He didn't mind her coming in and out at all and she often flaunted herself in front of him wearing really low cut tops and leaning over in front of him. She would sit at the kitchen table with her arms folded in front of her pushing her boobs up so it was hard not to notice. This infuriated me and I thought to myself you cheeky cow how dare you come into my home and do this in front of me with my husband.

On one occasion Katherine came round for a visit to see me and I believe this was on a Saturday which is usually a fairly busy day and a family day for us. So I was a little bit annoyed when she arrived. She always had a bad habit of never phoning before the visit to see if it was convenient. Being the friendly person that I am I just let her in and we sat down and I made us both a coffee. We spoke for a short while then Anthony walks in the kitchen and went and made himself a coffee. Anthony liked to talk to her and sat down conveniently next to her on the sofa opposite me. They sat very close together and I was on the other side of the room. My son was upstairs and came in and out frequently so I had to pay him attention. After a while I noticed their conversation was excluding me completely and they were both overtly flirting with each other. They were talking about Latin as they both had an interest in it. Katherine had achieved a Latin 'A' Level and I knew nothing of Latin so couldn't join in. It carried on for over an hour and she was wearing as per usual a low cut top and leaning in towards Anthony and he was enjoying the attention. They completely ignored me as if I wasn't there I found it somewhat annoying especially as our son was in and out. Her being there was now becoming irritating for me as I was trying to get on with my housework as I was back in work on the Monday as everyone else was. Eventually Anthony got up and went into the lounge and I was left in the kitchen with her. I confronted her about her behaviour and asked what the hell was she playing at and told her that I had thought she had come to see me for a coffee and not my husband. I also told her that I did not appreciate her flirting with my husband and it wasn't on. She immediately went very red in the face and surprisingly started to cry and blamed it on her sister's husband. I said "what are you playing at are you talking about our support worker called Stuart?" Katherine said in a childish voice and manner "No, no I don't fancy him" it's my brother in law Stuart. Well at that point I nearly left my body with shock. I couldn't believe what she had just said to me. To get herself out of the situation with me and Anthony she had told me a secret which I had not known about and couldn't believe it of her that she could have an affair with her twin sister's husband. She then went on to say it was all his fault and he had pestered her continually, as if, it takes two and she was very capable at saying what she did or did not want, she then stated that Stuart had told her he wished to start a new life with her in New Zealand and leave his wife and children behind. Basically just do a bunk together and leave everyone behind to pick up the pieces. I said to her as I was thinking about it, hang on, that takes a lot of planning so it must be a two way liaison with you both as how could he plan this without your consent? I then went on to say was this the reason why she and her twin sister Anne were not speaking to each other and it had been blamed on a Christmas meal. Katherine had blamed the relationship breakdown on an argument at the family Christmas meal. I then realised that this breakdown between them was far more serious than we had been led to believe. Katherine used this as a smokescreen to cloud the situation that was going on between my husband Anthony and her. I had suspected something was going on and I believe she knew it. I was really angry with her and her behaviour and told her so. I couldn't believe what she had done with her brother in law to her own sister and angrily said that I wasn't happy with her coming round to my home anymore after all this. However, she still kept coming and obviously didn't care what I felt and came to see me to tell me that the relationship was coming to an end with her brother in law. After she had left that day I felt I needed to confront Anthony, after Connor had gone to bed, about his behaviour with her in front of me. I told him I was not happy about it and they had made me feel really uncomfortable in my own home. His retort was, wait for it, that I was ruining his fun. I couldn't believe it, as Victor Meldrew would say. We argued most of the evening about this and it carried on into the Sunday. Anthony was decorating the front bedroom and I could feel the atmosphere which was very tense so I went into the room to discuss it with Anthony as it was affecting Connor and it wasn't fair on him. Anthony didn't like to be interrupted when he was decorating, I am laughing whilst I am thinking about this and wish I had put the paint over his head at the time, but I didn't, as usual he went absolutely mental screaming like a banshee. He said that after he had finished decorating the room he was going to leave me because I was ruining his fun again. He had said this to me many times but he had never left. I tried to placate him instead of fighting any more not standing up to him as I was still in the role of the victim. The root cause of all this was Katherine and her sneaky conniving behaviour I thought. It wasn't as she couldn't have an affair with Anthony unless he wanted it. She was in a void where her marriage to Dennis was over and her brother in law was on the scene but she couldn't have him all the time as he was married so I believed she had Anthony in her sights. He had definitely picked up her attentions at that point that she was interested in him. By Monday when I returned to work I had put it all behind me and just got on with my work. However, she seemed much more wary of me for a while as I don't think she thought I was capable of being like that with her. She too was quite a narcissistic individual too. Her twin sister Anne visited quite often but Katherine kept out of the way for a while and Anne never said a word about her life or her problems. Anne always painted a picture post card image of her relationship with her husband Stuart and her children. Yet the word on the local grapevine was that he was a womaniser but I couldn't and didn't ever mention that to Anne. I used to think she was so lucky however it was a complete fabrication of her life as Katherine had told me about her and Stuart and I also heard some time later that her eldest had been on drugs and her daughter was very sexually active and drank and smoked. So really her kids were no better than anyone else's and not the picture she liked to portray to everyone. I felt a little sad for her that she had to do that as no one is perfect and neither are their children. Both the twins actually thought they were something that they weren't and both had a fixation with money and on one occasion Anne actually asked how much would I be worth when my parents died. I found this question extremely insulting and thought what the hell has it to do with her. I was a bit shocked and told her I had no idea as I hadn't thought of it as they were both well and very happy. Very odd of her really. I was left wondering about that one as I always believed in life that there was a reason for everything that happens in our lives. I wondered if she was just nosy or not.

We all got on with our lives and life didn't really get much better for me really. I had no option but to speak with Katherine as she worked with me in the health service. Eventually we ended up on better terms as she stopped coming to my home and it all died down. Even Anne and Katherine started to speak again, about a year later, and I started to go to lunch with Anne and Katherine would just turn up without any invitation. I couldn't really say anything and ended up talking to her again socially. The visits started again to my home. When I look back on this Katherine would only come when she knew Anthony would be at work so this made me feel more comfortable with the relationship with her. I do believe now that she was being manipulative and she was trying to give me a false sense of security before she went for the jugular. She carefully commenced her plan of manipulation against me and was trying to drive me out of my marriage to Anthony. If I had an argument with Anthony I used to call her to talk with her about it. We used to meet up at the Health Club and have a drink, not always alcoholic at that point, and discuss the situation and she seemed to really get off on the drama of it all. I actually believed she was trying to help me, however, that wasn't the case as I now know she was after Anthony. Bear in mind this is a woman who stood up in court against me and said, in the internal work case, that she only saw me once a week socially! What a lying cow. I will tell you all about this in the following chapters. She was actually at my house nearly every day and this was not an invite by me. She also started to stay until Anthony came home again once she had gained my confidence again. Once again she was turning up to our home on Saturdays and used to once again sit talking to Anthony for most of the afternoon.

Katherine was rather silly really that in her evidence to the internal investigation at work she stated that she only met once a week socially. Now this is a complete lie as I do have a witness that will state that this is not the truth. This is my dear friend Laney and she will give evidence that she saw her car outside my house nearly every day when she came home from work or when she was at home when she had finished her job. Laney was also a witness to discussions with Katherine and myself in my home about the bruises I had and the violence that Laney had witnessed. Other neighbours have also given written statements to say the same. This all went to the professional body in London and they didn't take any notice whatsoever of the evidence put in front of them.

I had started to become suspicious on occasions as I often wondered how she knew snippets of information about me as I had never told her and she often slipped up in her eagerness to get me into trouble whilst seeming helpful and understanding to me. She was a very clever manipulator just like Anthony. They say like attracts like and it was very true in this case. Over the years this all came to light and reflecting back she was instrumental in the last four violent serious situations I found myself in within my marriage.

Over time I was tired of my daughter not being allowed to visit me with her little boys and I often missed them and had asked and asked Anthony to allow my daughter and her two children to visit me at our home. The answer was always no on each occasion. I always tried to time my requests to him when I felt he was in a good mood but that didn't work either. I had to continue to visit them at their home but I felt very strongly about this situation and that it was wicked of him to do this to me. I just didn't mention it to him again as I knew I wouldn't get anywhere he was a total control freak and I was terrified of him.

My friend Anne suggested that we should go out for an evening and it sounded good so I was up for that. We were going into Hale, Cheshire, and picking her friend Edna up on the way. We arrived at the Wine Bar in Hale and to my surprise Katherine was there. We had a good evening and we were all drinking even though she was driving. Yes she was driving whilst under the influence of alcohol but she didn't get caught. Throughout the evening I had a good conversation with Edna and I mentioned my grandchildren and how I wasn't allowed to have them at our home. She was astonished that my husband had refused to allow my daughter and grandchildren into our home. She was horrified and could not believe that I was going along with this and allowing it to happen. I agreed with her and told her I had been trying for a long time and he would not relent and I didn't want to put her in the position of coming to our home and being treated horribly by Anthony as he had already thrown her out. This conversation hit home and left me with feelings of weakness and inadequacy that I was not able to stand up to Anthony.

We all had a lot to drink during the evening and were all suitably jolly and I felt quite brave with the alcohol inside me so when I arrived home I approached Anthony about the subject yet again. I told him that I was having my family in my house and as it was half my house and that he basically couldn't stop me. This didn't do me any good it set off like a lit torch to paper and he erupted like a volcano yet again. I thought OMG here we go again and ran into the kitchen to get away from him as I saw the anger in his face which was contorted like a rabid animal. I managed to escape into the kitchen but he came at me and threw me onto the chair, climbed on top of me, and again I felt him put his hands around my throat and started to strangle me. As I felt the choking sensation I began feeling light headed and I thought OMG he is going to kill me. I managed to turn my head towards his shoulder and I bit him hard on the top of his arm to try to get him off me. It worked because I really had hurt him in self-defence and he jumped off me and went around to the far side of the kitchen near the patio doors. I approached him releasing my fear and telling him he was not to touch me again and that I was having my grandchildren in my own home and he wouldn't stop me. He then again grabbed me by the top of my arms and threw me across the kitchen straight into a shelf. The shelf had metal knobs on it and this stuck in my head and I bled everywhere in the kitchen. I saw a big circle of blood on the floor and I remember this well. I also remember thinking what the hell had he done to me.

I was so terrified I didn't say a word I got up and ran out of the house and went to my neighbour Della Windel who lived in the next road. I arrived at her house confused, distressed and covered in blood and their faces looked horrified as I stood on their doorstep. Della put me in her car and took me to Treeford General. This was the 26 February 2011. They stuck my scalp back on to my head in A & E and I sat in triage really distressed and alleged to the medical staff that I had suffered constant abuse over many years. This has been recorded in my medical notes. Della Windel then took me back to her house where her husband was waiting for us. He had been in the kitchen at their home when I had arrived. Della didn't want me to go home but I said I had to get it sorted out and that we couldn't carry on like this.

I walked back to my house and as I came around the corner I saw a police vehicle outside my home. I wondered who had called them as it wasn't me or Della. I went into the house, this was hours and hours after the attack, and was fairly with it by then. There were two police officers in my house in the kitchen and Anthony was not there. The police had taken him away as I found out from them that he had accused me of biting him which I had. They hadn't got the full circumstances though only his version which was quite sneaky of him to have called them

77

in blaming me. I tried to explain the situation to the two police-men and they said they would keep him in the cells overnight for him to calm down. I didn't press charges against him as I was too frightened and didn't know which way to go. The police just left me in the house after having given a statement and I did not feel supported by the two policemen. Anthony was such a good liar and had said that I had attacked him and bitten him and all he was doing was defending himself against me.

The next day it was quite late in the afternoon Anthony came home and quite surprisingly he was quite remorseful about my head injury. I also found two tea towels soaking with blood hid-den in the garage. Obviously, he had hidden these from the po-lice and cleaned the kitchen so it looked like there was no blood. All this just so I didn't have to meet my daughter and kids on park benches or in supermarkets and just wanted them to be able to visit. I used to visit her at her home but felt uncomfortable as Nige was there as he wasn't working at that time. This is why I was paying for their flat.

For the next few months I felt numbness in my hands and my neck was stiff. Throughout all of this I was trying to work. He actually apologised to me after this incident and I found the courage to stand up to him and I told him that I would be hav-ing my family in my home as it's only once a week and to my astonishment he relented and agreed. I also said I wanted him to apologise to my daughter for not letting her in the house. He said that he would and was acting like a sulky kid. When he was feeling guilty he was more pliable and I came out of this with a very positive resolution. I told my daughter the good news but never told her what had happened and she visited Friday after-noons with the babies and was always gone before he got home anyway. On one occasion he came home when they were still there and he went over to Rachel and apologised and kissed her on the cheek I nearly fell over with the shock. However, he might have said hello to them but he never did and didn't take any in-terest or did anything with them. I always made sure the house was cleaned after their visit so he had nothing to moan about.

The next few months were the calm before the storm and I felt at last everything was being sorted out. The period of calm lasted about three months before the storm, which actually realistically was a bad rainfall. He suggested in a calm manner that I should be the one going to see Rachel at her house as she was no longer at the flat. They were renting a property in Stockport now just off the motorway not really very nice but all they could afford and was suitable for children but they didn't have good neighbours. I told him that if I had to drive to Stockport and back on a Friday afternoon it would be quite hectic as the traffic was horrendous on Fridays and most of the day would be gone. I explained all this to him and I also had Connor to look after but he still kept on about it all the time. I wished he would just give up and go away.

At this time he was working hard and doing his Master's degree and he was not helping with the family and house as he was too busy. I only had Thursdays off and Friday was spent with my daughter and her family. Thursdays were really busy as I had to take his clothes to the dry cleaners or take ironing to the service. Then there was the housework, cooking and all the shopping and I often worked at weekends Saturday or Sunday every now and again. However, Anthony played squash nearly every evening for at least two hours followed by a beer or two before driving home at about 8pm. He would never be in before 8pm in the evenings unless we were going out to the pub with his friends. On a Wednesday he went to a local university to study for his Master's degree. He studied on Saturday and Sunday afternoons. When there was good weather and he had any spare time he would be off on his motorbike. Friday nights were nearly always spent with his mates in the pub. Sunday evenings he was always at the pub with his friends after his study time. I only saw Anthony for one and a half hours on a Monday evening for a quiz night with his friends when he was around otherwise on Monday he said he would be working. He was often away on a Monday night saying it was for work. On a Thursday evening I would see him for another hour and a half at the pub with his friends. All he talked about at the pub was himself and his degree. People looked really bored and he never stopped talking about it. Saturday evenings he was at home with me. He would make a nice Thai meal for us and I have to admit he was quite a good cook. This is the sum total of a full week with my husband. Occasionally he would go and watch Connor play football instead of playing squash. In saying this I mean if his partner couldn't play that day he would take Connor and watch the game. My life was actually a real drudge as he had isolated me from my friends with only Anne coming to visit me. I believe she truly didn't like Anthony but Katherine did.

It eventually came to light that Anthony would tell Katherine whatever I told her about him was lies and I was telling stories about him. She obviously believed him and he had her convinced about me. This also had an impact with other people not believing me when I told them what Anthony was like and what he did to me. He always undermined me in front of my friends and his and made me out to be a very lazy person which was quite the opposite. I was exhausted and run ragged as I was continually drained trying to make sure the home was up to his standards and when I thought I had actually met them he always found fault with something. If I put my bag down anywhere he would always comment and tell me to move it. He always made below the belt comments about me and in front of Connor and anyone who happened to be around. He delighted in humiliating me in front of others and this hurt me so much and caused me so much pain. I would always try to defend myself and mention what I actually did. He would then undermine me again and I found this behaviour of his constantly exhausting. He made me feel ugly and overweight. He said I wasn't doing enough exercise and I was letting myself go. I had started to suffer with not sleeping, eating less and becoming very anxious. I had also started to drink more. I decided to spend some money on myself and go and get my hair done. I made an appointment at the hairdressers and she did a lovely cut and put some colours through my hair and I felt and looked good and this elated me and raised my spirits. I felt maybe he would think I looked attractive. I had lost some weight and had my hair done and really felt good about myself. He was in the lounge when I got home, working on his degree, and I went in and said that I'd had my hair done. Not making any positive comments he said "How much did that cost you?" cheeky pig, the nerve of the man, as he was paying three hundred and eighty five pounds a month for his motorbike. That was nearly another mortgage. Basically he wasn't interested in me or anything I was trying to do to salvage our marriage. He spent most of his time talking about this woman at university who was also doing a degree. He seemed infatuated with her intelligence. I believe he was having an affair with her. I mentioned her earlier on about the wedding we went to and she was there and came over and suggested to me that I go home. I believe that Anthony had invited that woman to the evening reception of the wedding to deliberately be offensive towards me.

The 17th October 2011 I walked out of the house with my pink handbag in my hand and to say I was confused is a massive understatement. I went to the local shop and bought a bottle of wine and sat in the grounds of Treeford General, down by the side of the hospital. No one could see me sitting there and I just drank and drank. Something had happened that day which totally traumatised me and I think I perhaps drank at least two to three bottles of wine. The Police picked me up outside someone's house, not sure who they were, and they drove me to my mum's in Marple Bridge. I stated to the policeman that on one hand my husband was wonderful and yet was a total bastard. I was confused with his behaviour as he had what seemed to be a split personality and I told them that he had been hitting me. They carried out a vulnerable assessment on me but yet did nothing to help me. I spent the next two to three days at my mum's house in bed. My brother John and his son Daniel came to visit and asked me what had been going on and it all came out that he was hurting me. I told them how I felt so humiliated, deflated and that I just couldn't cope anymore and was drinking more and more to blot out the pain and hurt that was like searing pain through my body.

My brother was really unhappy about the situation. He said I should see a solicitor and was astonished that Anthony had not phoned anyone to check on me. I had also walked off from the bench at Treeford General without my handbag and I had left it there. Anthony told my brother that he had not known where I was and that I had been drinking. Anthony had got my pink handbag as someone found it and looked inside and got my address and had taken it to the house. I had left a reading from a Medium who worked in the Treeford Centre in the pink bag. Which Anthony had read and retained and kept in a file of his. The reading had stated that Anthony was seeing lots of other women and was violent towards me. So he would have seen this but as you can imagine when I finally went back home after I rang him to come and get me as I had to get back to work. There was no conversation and the atmosphere in the car was very tense. He said to me, "Now look what you've done. People can now see what you are like". Always blaming me and saying I was a total mess. He never mentioned what he had done to me or threatened to do. He then went on to say that he had moved his money over to a new account and that I would have to pay all the bills from my money and he would top up what was necessary. So he was trying to get my money as well. It was alright for him to spend thirty six pounds each on two bottles of wine each week for himself but he wanted to stop me spending on what I wanted. He was making my money the main money for the household bills and day-to-day living and he said I was not allowed to question him. He also said that if my behaviour did not improve that this was the way it was always going to be because he couldn't trust me. In reality he was ferreting away his money and because I was so scared of him I put all my money in and used it on the house. I couldn't see a way out of this at that time. This was in October 2011 and the next few months of my life were so very difficult. I felt so strongly that he was seeing other women and basically either ignored me when Connor was around and was very aggressive when Connor was not around. I barely spoke any words at all during this time. This went on and on for months and I was going further and further into myself and was trying to find friendships and was relying on Katherine and meeting up with her. In hindsight I was telling her everything and Anthony was finding out what I had said and yet she denied telling him. How could he possibly know everything that I had said to her nearly word for word if she hadn't told him?

The week before the 10 January 2012 where I nearly died, Anthony had been invited to go to Amsterdam for a long weekend. They were going very early on the Saturday and returning on the Tuesday. The Friday night before he had got so drunk he could hardly walk so when the taxi arrived on the Saturday morning he didn't feel like going. The group of lads were all in the cab waiting for him and there was a bang on the door and I said to Anthony that his taxi was here. I went to the door and told them he was just getting ready and he got into the taxi and left for his jolly Amsterdam trip.

That morning Connor had asked me to show him how to make scrambled eggs which I did. We enjoyed our breakfast together. Katherine had arranged to meet up with me Saturday lunchtime and Connor had gone to one of his friend's houses. Katherine arrived and she took me out and we had a couple of drinks. She knew I had a problem, however, she just she kept getting me drink after drink which I obviously didn't turn down. I got home from our lunch at about six-ish and just in time to take a call from Anthony in Amsterdam. He was drunk and was taunting me about going out to the red light district to have some fun. Telling me what he fancied doing with all the gorgeous girls that were spread-eagled across the front of the windows to display their bodies. This upset me and really hurt deep down and yet again I turned to the bottle to down my sorrows not a good thing to do as I had to work on the Sunday. I coped quite well throughout the day but there was evidence that I had not written my notes up properly as I wasn't thinking straight at all and I had also left my bleep as I'd taken it out of my pocket and just left it somewhere. So work wasn't happy with me at all but this didn't come out until months later. I can't blame them either. On Monday 9th I rang in work sick. I could not carry on really and I don't remember much of the Monday or the Tuesday. Katherine turned up and she had called him in Amsterdam so, obviously, had my husband's phone number. He told me this at a later date. I was completely out of it at this point and was terrified of him. He phoned me when he arrived back in the UK and before he had got home to tell me he was on his way and was going to sort me out. I was terrified and when he came through the door he came into the kitchen he was screaming at me. I ran up into the bedroom and thought I would climb down the drainpipe and get out before he could beat the shit out of me again. He knew what I had been doing as Katherine had phoned him and told him. She had done this on purpose. If she had cared at all about me she would have tried to help me not set me up for yet another beating. I climbed out of the window and was inching down to get to the drainpipe and was aware he was after me. I slipped and went flying on to the top of my car which was about 3 metres below and bounced off onto the driveway. I fractured my right wrist and dislocated my right shoulder and fractured my back. I had lost consciousness on the driveway so Anthony had to call an ambulance. I remember waking up in A&E and stating that I believed all of my problems arose from my toxic relationship with my husband. I have found out since from my neighbours that Anthony came out and took photos of me on the floor whilst I was unconscious. The ambulance didn't move from outside the house for twenty minutes and Anthony had just walked off and gone inside the house and left me on my own in the ambulance. The paramedics knocked on the door and asked Anthony if he was aware that his wife had no pulse and did he want to come to the hospital with me. My neighbours told me that Anthony just ignored them and walked back in the house saying he had to go and tidy up the mess I had made in the house. When I woke up in A&E, I had gas and air and remember screaming with the pain when they put my elbow back in. I had dislocated it during the fall. I was told by the hospital staff that my husband had not telephoned to see if I had died or not. I was later transferred to a ward where I had investigations and x-rays on my wrist and my back. People came to talk to me because they thought I had tried to commit suicide which I had to laugh at really as I was actually trying to get away from Anthony. Even my family thought I had tried to commit suicide because they hadn't known what was happening in my life. I then also had to go through a mental health assessment to see if I was bonkers or not. The records actually state "she believes all problems are sourced from her relationship with her husband". Luckily for me they decided that I wasn't. I was quite terrified as I am sure that Anthony would have really liked me to have died or been committed; he would have been rid of me and been able to keep the house, control my son, and have all the money to himself. As soon as he had got me out of my own house he moved another woman in to my home who he had played squash with and whom I had suspected was having an affair with him. Interestingly enough my husband and Connor came into the hospital to bring me in some toiletries as I had nothing only what I had on. So he brought me a toothbrush with no toothpaste, old top and bottoms that didn't even match and a hairbrush. I told him that I was frightened at going down for surgery and all he could say was that it was my own fault and then left. I had been advised by the medical staff that once I was classed as medically fit I would be going down for surgery on my arm. Anthony didn't come back to visit whilst I was in the hospital for a week. My mum and Clive, one of my brothers, came to visit me, my daughter Rachel came to see me, my friend Jane Heathfield also came and one of my work colleagues who was also my friend popped in to see me. The two people that did not come to see me were Katherine and Anne. I didn't receive a card from them or any communication. I wonder why? When I was discharged, Anthony had to come and pick me up as I couldn't go home on my own. My family were still unsure of my mental state and even they were confused about my actions but they were supporting me now and that was important for me.

There was also an additional instance that led me to try to escape from my home. Anthony had locked me in the house and I was really scared of him coming back so I rang my friend who had been a probation officer and understood some of his behaviour. I told her I was distressed and Anthony had locked me in the house, locking all doors and taking the keys with him. She was concerned enough to get in touch with my brother Richard who came over with Molly my friend. They told me to open a window, which I did, and they helped me get out as the bay windows were very high and they took me to my mum's house. I do not think that either my brother or my friend were happy with me at that time as I had obviously interrupted their day. They made me feel safe though. He actually came to pick me up from my mum's house and came inside. He said to my mum before she could even open her mouth that everything Tyff says about me is lies, all lies and he kept repeating this. My mum was only a small lady in stature, she stood up and told him that he had no right to lock me in the house and take the keys with him and remove all my money. She banged on the table at the same time and I had never seen her like this ever. He stood there with his mouth open and said nothing. He took it out on me in the car on the way home as he yet again gave me a barrage of abuse and told me it was my fault. He said he was trying to protect me from myself. I said to him that if he was so worried, why hadn't he tried to get me some help? He had never tried to help, he was the problem and the reason why I turned to alcohol. He never once suggested that I should get help he just kept setting me up for a big fall. He was very manipulative and controlling and Katherine and Anthony were in cahoots, planning carefully to get rid of me. She was forever asking me to go out drinking with her and then set me up with Anthony. Telling him when I had had a drink and each time he found out I got a beating for it. Not that he needed an excuse, he would just invent something. He had to have a reason though and it was always me that had made him do it. He was very busy planning and seeing other women. Because I was drunk all the time she told everyone that I was making everything up about Anthony so no one actually ever believed me. They always believed her because she was sober when she told everyone about me. They hadn't seen her drunk as she had been on hundreds of occasions and I had to look after her to stop her from choking on her vomit she was so bad. Anthony too, he was a big drinker, but he never got caught and no one ever saw him either. I am not trying to blame anyone else but just trying to say that they both made such a big deal to everyone that I was a raving drunk who couldn't be trusted and told lies. That's all they ever said to anyone.

The problems I had within my marriage and my drinking became progressively worse over the years. So no doubt you may be able to understand why I was really shocked when Anthony said should we go away on holiday to Arran as he liked it there. Connor was going away for a week on an adventure holiday to Spain so Anthony had said we couldn't afford to go abroad. I wasn't too happy about going on holiday with him on my own and I was at this point of not drinking to try to get everything back on track. We had been to Arran previously and had a lovely time. I agreed to go away and packed for Connor and ourselves. The luggage was heavy as we had to pack for a walking holiday and had to take the appropriate clothing with us. Connor went off on his holiday with school and we went off to Arran. The journey seemed fine with no arguments and the hotel was The Burlington where we had stayed before. We went to a local shop the first day as I had said the coat I had was far too heavy for walking up the mountain and I wanted to get one that was specific for the purpose. There was a coat in the sale which was £29.00 and was much better for me and we also bought two walking sticks. I felt the hostility towards me as I didn't feel he wanted to buy this coat for me. He looked agitated and his eyes looked very angry. With them being so very dark he looked quite evil on occasions and scary. I felt the holiday was to show Connor our son how good he was taking me on holiday. I had become very suspicious as to why he did these things. We went off to the local bar each evening where they served excellent food at a good price. We really enjoyed it and I was the chauffeur every night as I wasn't drinking. Anthony drank each night at the pub. We had made an earlier agreement that no alcohol would be brought into our house and not drank in front of me. So this soon changed within a week of his commitment to me. He was drinking lager each evening. On the first day of the holiday we went shopping and he bought a large box of wine and I wasn't very happy about this at all. At the end of each day he had had three pints and he would drink glass after glass of wine whilst we played scrabble and he always won. I asked once if we could play chess as I was really good at that but he would never agree as he couldn't beat me. We always had to do what Anthony wanted to do. I was really unhappy about the wine situation and found it really uncomfortable to watch his drinking in the hotel bedroom. After his drinking session he would lock the wine box up in his suitcase so that I couldn't touch it. This was all deliberate and I knew what he was doing and I kept to my promise and I never drank on the holiday. We went for a walk one day to one of the Tarns, a little lake, and I always remember seeing a great big snake which came right across our path when we were walking up. I knew it was an adder but it caused no harm we just stood there and let it go on its way. When we got to the top of the Tarn the view was absolutely stunning and the water was clear and still and we sat and had our lunch. It was so peaceful it was like the lull before the storm I felt everything was too calm. I somehow had this inner knowing and knew this day that this marriage is over and I didn't trust him.

The medium at the Treeford Centre had told me he was seeing other women and was preparing to leave me and we would go on a holiday just before it would happen. These words resonated through my head. She was always so precise and accurate with her evidence. Everything else she had said had turned out to be true. This was the last holiday we ever had together and I felt very sad that day and I knew inside it was over. We walked back down to the hotel and had a meal out that evening. We did the same things as we had done nearly every night apart from one when we had gone to see a local play. Again this evening he had drunk himself in to a bit of a stupor and then locked up his wine. I felt quite tired and the TV was still on really loud so I just said would he mind very much turning the TV down a little so I could sleep. He grudgingly adjusted it a minute amount. I didn't want to antagonise him so I just turned over in bed to go to sleep. He got into bed and was lying next to me when he sat up and had his back to me on the edge of the bed. I could feel the energy change; it was horrible as I had experienced this so many times before. I was now becoming really scared as I also knew what he was capable of. My mind quickly went back to the Greece episode where I had tried to get away and other times where I had tried to get away. So I just lay there kind of paralysed and did nothing knowing he would hit me if I tried to get out of the room. I stayed still all night and was too scared to get out of bed even for the toilet. In the morning I was desperate to go to the toilet so I was starting to get out of the bed and he jumped up quickly saying he needed the toilet first. So I had to go downstairs in my pyjamas to use the hotel toilets. Nothing was said during breakfast. We had loaded up the car and were about to set off and he said why don't you drive. We didn't have a sat nav so I said I don't know the way home so he drove home. We arrived home on the 30th August 2012 and the Sunday was pretty non- descript as I was just washing and ironing etc. and getting everything ready for the return to work and Connor's arrival on Monday. Monday morning I said to Anthony that we needed to keep an eye on our phones as the school would be advising us by text the time they were arriving back at the school and we would have to go to pick him up. Anthony immediately said you don't have to come. I said that I wanted to come. When it was time to go after we had received the text I just went and got in the car. Again I could feel this terrible energy as this was not what he wanted as he didn't really want anyone to see me normal and happy. When we arrived at the school he just jumped out of the car and left me in the car. That evening I unpacked Connor's case and then busied myself sorting it all out. It was

quite funny I had to laugh as I had packed eight pairs of underwear for Connor and there were seven clean pairs left so he must
have just worn the one pair for the whole holiday and he must
have got them wet. Boys will be boys I thought. September was
approaching and Connor was back to school and cycling there
with his friend Mark as he was becoming more independent. I
noticed that Mark was cycling around to our house putting his
bike in our garage and then Anthony was taking them to school.
So Connor was trying to be independent and Anthony was trying to take that away from him to have power and control over
Connor and it also made Anthony look good to everyone around
us. But the problem was that it meant that Connor and his friend
had to walk back to our house. So I offered to come and pick
Connor and Mark up from school whenever I could. Not long
after my offer Anthony must have had an issue with me picking
them up. So Anthony would turn up at the same time as me or
even before and pick up the boys. When I arrived at the school
Anthony was already there and Connor was getting in the car.
He told Connor that I was getting mixed up and was going bonkers and why had she come to pick you up today when she knew
I was coming for you. However, that wasn't the case, Anthony set me up with my son and it was all about ruining the relationship I had with my son. It was all part of his game trying to
make me seem mentally ill and turn my son against me this was
a deliberate act. The picture he painted to Connor was that I was
either confused, stupid or had no memory of what he had discussed with me and would always put me down in front of him
to make out I was stupid. He would buy lots of expensive things
for Connor and was also painting this picture to Mark. A few
weeks later, Anthony was going to stay away overnight on business, or so he said, and he asked Mark if Connor could stay with
him as he didn't trust me. He had already painted the picture by
turning up at school even though he had to leave work early to
do so. He normally didn't finish until four thirty and the school
finished at three fifteen and that was in Manchester so it would
take him thirty minutes to get there. So Anthony was now ma-

nipulating Mark and his mother into thinking that I was mad and stupid and that Connor was not safe with me. I hadn't been drinking through all of this and had been off the booze for eight months. So I was back to my old self apart from the fear of him.

On my birthday the 18th September, I received a card from Anthony. It was a cheap crap card and this time he had just written best wishes when previously he had always put all my love always Anthony. A few days before my birthday he had asked me what I would like as a present which he had never done before and always surprised me. I said I needed a couple of cardigans and that's exactly what I got. He didn't take me out for a meal like he always did. This upset served as a catalyst for me drinking again and I did start having the odd glass of wine behind his back. However, I could put it down and pick it up again without any problems and I was still working and had no problems at work at all. October approached where the wedding invite came which I have spoken about earlier. I felt at this time he was definitely seeing someone else and although I didn't drink on this weekend he drank like a fish. I got him home after the wedding and he was so drunk he fell out of bed and I just left him on the floor. He must have got up in the night being cold and got himself back in bed. He only did this when Connor couldn't see it but highlighted what I did. He became more and more abusive to me and he would push me about. I had a lot of bruises on my arms and I had mentioned this to Anne my friend. It all came to a climax when I drank too much one weekend as he was abusing me in the bedroom. He was doing things to me that he had never done in our twenty years together. I was truly traumatised by one of the things he did and he felt he could do anything he liked to me and get away with it. He knew I wouldn't like it and knew I didn't like it and didn't agree to it and to me it was like being raped. He wasn't holding me down or anything like that but I said I didn't want to do it and I did not enjoy it. He felt he could get away with it at the time because I was drinking again. The next event was on a Saturday and my son was in the house and I had been drinking and he was being very aggressive and verbally abusive and I was trying to get away from him via the side door in the hallway connecting to the garage. I actually got into the garage and he grabbed me and threw me on the floor which was concrete and he sat on top of me. He held my head pushing me down into the concrete floor for at least an hour. I was shouting and screaming for him to get off me as I could hardly breathe. Connor came into the garage and saw what was going on and Anthony immediately told Connor that he was doing this because it was my fault as I had been drinking again and that's what made him violent towards me. Eventually he got off me and I went up to my bedroom and never came out. I still managed to get to work the next day and I sobered up and went to see a solicitor and was petitioning for a divorce. I didn't tell Anthony at this time and took some of his payslips for information purposes. Both Katherine and Anne knew I was divorcing him on the grounds of domestic violence so they were well aware of what was going on and that he was hurting me. They knew how distressed I was by all of this. I started to buy the ready-made meals that didn't need a fridge or to be warmed up with crisps and a few other bits and pieces. I had a plan how I could stay at work and keep out of his way. He would be particularly nasty to me verbally before I went to work to try to upset me and cause me further problems. My plan of action was to feed myself so I didn't have to go near him at any time. I also started. in the last few weeks whilst I was still working, to get up half an hour earlier than him so I didn't have to see him. He had moved out of my bedroom but still came in each morning for his clothes and was nasty to me. Without his verbal abuse I felt I could focus on my job better. I arrived at the Health Centre in the mornings before they had even opened the doors to the building and I often met Shirley Ascott who was the occupational therapist and was best friends with my friend Katherine. She commented that it was odd to see me so early in the morning. I told her that I had to leave the house before that man could abuse me and that I was now trying to get away from him by petitioning for divorce. As soon as I got in from work I would make tea for me and Connor and would eat it very quickly so I could go up to my bedroom to avoid him. Anne was coming round frequently to see if I was ok and she knew that I was going straight up to my bedroom and she knew all about what was happening at the time. She would also have told Katherine about it therefore she would have been aware about my circumstances. I would be up in my bedroom from around six thirty and sometimes he didn't come home until nine. If he did come in I would hide under the bedclothes as I was so terrified that he would eventually kill me. When we did ever meet in the kitchen or elsewhere in our home he would question me about every penny I spent even though it was my money that was going into the account as he had his own account as I said earlier. He made me write down on a list in the kitchen every single penny that I spent and he actually put down what he had spent quite bizarre really. The only thing I put on the list was that I had bought a piece of luggage worth fifty pounds that was my indicator to him that I was leaving and Connor saw that note and wrote *Ha Ha No* on it. I was in bed and I could hear Anthony coming up the stairs like a bolt of lightning he stormed into the bedroom and went mental with me saying how dare I spend fifty pounds, of my own money, on a piece of luggage. I thought he was going to blow up he was so angry and red faced. I told him that it was only a joke and I hadn't actually bought a suitcase but I thought it was absolutely ludicrous to be having to write everything down at his command. I also, at this point, tried to hide some money in a black purse I had. He was watching every penny I spent probably as I drank or because he knew I was going to leave. I had been putting some money away for my escape so I had money for food and fuel. I felt like I was trying to survive. One day he came into the bedroom and pulled all the drawers out and contents from the wardrobe and he found my stash of what was a small amount of money and took it away. My heart sank with dismay and I felt totally hopeless at that point. I thought to myself how the hell did he know about that. I remember mentioning this to either Katherine or Anne so it must have come from them.

I had started staying at my mums every weekend and the only time I was in that house was when I had to go to work. My mum was happy as I wasn't drinking at her house at that time as I felt I was in a safe environment.

I had started proceedings with the solicitor and was still living at home. I went to the works Christmas party which was held at the Church Hotel and Katherine had suggested that I stay at her house as it was only walking distance from the hotel. I did go, I don't know why and I remember I was wearing a black polka dot dress. I was at a very low point and had been traumatised by the endless years of abuse. I probably shouldn't have gone as we both drank too much that evening. We went back to Katherine's home and I stayed up all night in my dress whilst she went off to bed. It was an evening where my brain was assimilating all the events of the many years of hurt and abuse. The morning came and Katherine got up and came down the stairs but I was still feeling traumatised and I knew I could not go back to my home in case he smelt or knew I had been drinking. I told Katherine I was not fit to drive home and I pleaded with her to please not take me home and could I not stay at her house that day. I told her if he knows that I have been drinking then he will hurt me again and she flatly refused to let me stay as she said she was playing tennis that day at the Health Club. What kind of friend was this I asked myself with a relationship spanning twenty years or more you would have thought she would have been a little bit more compassionate yet she made me get in the car and told me she was taking me home and I didn't really have any choice in the matter. Just before we left however, she said she needed to go to the loo (*this must have been to phone Anthony to let him know*). We went on our way and thirty minutes later arrived at my house I opened the door and the alarm was on so I went in to turn it off with the keypad. Anthony's car was not there as he often went to watch Connor play football on a Saturday morning so he wouldn't have known I had come home or had a drink unless someone had secretly let him know. As I was just turning the alarm off with my glasses on and Katherine was stood in the hallway waiting for me to turn it off Anthony arrived and walked straight in past Katherine in the doorway and as I lifted my head up to look I received a direct punch into my face with my glasses on. OMG that hurt you bastard and I sustained a gash over the bridge of my nose and I went flying down the hall and landed on my right arm which was the one that had been previously injured on one of my escape attempts. At no point did my so called friend do or say anything to help she just stood there and watched. She had a twisted grin on her face as if she actually loathed me. I was shocked to see this. I got up quickly and ran up to the bedroom and stayed there and heard them talking downstairs and then she just left. I watched her leave and she didn't look back at all, not even to check I was alright. I noticed that there were two children playing outside my neighbour's directly opposite to our house who must have witnessed something and of course Katherine's car was also there. I was now certain she had been having an affair and had set me up for him to come back and catch me and punish me. It was quite apparent that they had both set me up.

That evening I left the house and walked for a long time trying to clear my brain. A group of lads about five of them in all saw me and kindly said who has hit you in your face and shall we go and get him for you. I said there was no point as no one believed me. I felt so low, empty and lonely but had to get myself sorted for work on Monday as I was desperately trying to hold onto my job whilst trying to sort my head out. I was in triage on the Monday and I had put heavy makeup on to try and hide the cut but one of the support workers had come in to do some photocopying and she said hello to me and asked me if I was alright and what was the gash on my head. So she did witness it but I said that I had just banged myself and she looked at me in disbelief and left it there. I was so confused about everything even my own identity as a person I was a woman who had been abused but had no understanding of what had happened to me and that I was in the middle of a very confusing mess. I didn't even know what day it was I was just holding on.

I had been going for counselling to get help but I had only just started some of the counselling which was how to live with an abusive man and make it work. You see what a fool I was actually trying to make my marriage work. I was told that it could take up to eleven years to get past it but when you are actually in it you are so confused you are in so much danger that you are too frightened to do anything in case he kills you.

The following week I was in my bedroom again and he had been coming in for days each evening antagonising me so I had asked him to move his clothes out of the bedroom as I didn't want him in there anymore but I was so ill at that point I could hardly function properly. He didn't move them so after many requests and me having quite a few glasses of wine I threw all of his clothes onto the landing together with his gold bracelet. When I was doing this my son Connor had come out of his bedroom onto the landing and was watching and to my horror was filming me quite obviously evidence of my behaviour for his dad. He had been told to take photos of anything I did and Anthony used to film me too. Anthony quite often came into my room and took photos of me in bed to support his claims that I was mad and was away with the fairies. I shouted to Connor that his dad had raped me of my life and that I may be a drinker but he was the culprit and Connor took a video of this. I went back into my bedroom in my pyjamas and Connor had rang his dad and apparently he had rung the police and four large police officers, three men and a woman, came into my bedroom and they took me out of bed saying that I was disturbing the peace in my own home. I couldn't believe what was happening. I was trying to explain to them what had been happening and showed them the food in the cupboard and told them I was living out of my bedroom because I was terrified of Anthony. The police woman just threw some clothes in a bag. I had no hairbrush or toothbrush as they carted me off in hand cuffs into the back of the police van. I was wearing my pyjamas at the time and it was freezing cold in the back of the van. I hadn't done anything but thrown his clothes out of my bedroom because he wouldn't and he refused to stay out of my bedroom. He actually slept in the other bedroom and there was a spare shower room but he insisted on having his shower in my bedroom (previously our joint bedroom) saying that it was his shower. They took me to the police station where I had to stay overnight in a cell and had to ask for a blanket because I was so cold. I was charged with disturbing the peace in my own home and had to go to court the next day. I was allowed to put the clothes on which had been already worn I couldn't even brush my teeth or comb my hair. They did not listen to me at all when I tried to explain and tell them the truth. I couldn't believe what was happening to me how he had managed to do this he had even said he was going to get me committed to a mental health institution. I wasn't mentally ill I was just terrified of him and no one would believe me and I can say this now I was an alcoholic at that time. He wanted me out of his life but didn't want to part with the house or his money. The home was mine before he came into my life. At this point I had been abused for about twenty years as the first three years he was such a lovely husband. The next morning after the court case where I had to appear with no make-up, no toothbrush and some old clothes they took which didn't match so you can imagine what I looked like in front of a judge. I was charged with disturbing the peace in my own home without any evidence being provided by Anthony as he didn't come to the court. I tried to explain what had happened in the two minute time slot I had been given by them and I was given a fine which I had to pay. I wasn't allowed to disturb the peace again for at least six months. It didn't matter that my husband could beat the living shit out of me for the past seventeen years and punch me in front of people at all as I was not believed he was such a convincing liar such as sociopaths are. After the court case I was allowed out and had just enough money to get a taxi home. In the taxi everything was going around in my mind that I had just received a fine and a six months court order not to breach the peace again. It didn't matter that he had been breaching the peace continuously for seventeen years with his violent, aggressive, mentally demeaning behaviour towards me. Little did I know that this would be the last day of my life in my home? When I arrived home I approached my front door and I couldn't get in so I rang the doorbell. I looked a complete wreck at the time because the clothes the police had shoved in the bag didn't even match, as I said I had no hairbrush or toothbrush. Anthony came to the front door and he just waved me to go away. I noticed a car parked up outside my home which I thought was odd. So I walked around the back of my home as I needed some clothes and my work clothes and toiletries. It was obvious that it was not his intention to let me in to get anything. I looked through the patio doors into my kitchen and there was a woman sat in one of our cream leather chairs. I banged on the patio door to get her attention as this was my own home and yet I wasn't allowed in it. She spoke to Anthony and after a few minutes he did actually open the door and so I was let in. I asked who this woman was in my home. I was told she was the social worker that he had previously mentioned to me. He had told me that there was a case conference about me to get me committed the previous week. I had telephoned her myself the previous week. She had said to me on the phone she couldn't have had a case conference as she was on annual leave which I have mentioned earlier. The social worker said that Anthony had taken legal advice and that I had to leave my home. No meetings no reasons just that he had taken legal advice. *Another stitch up* I thought to myself. He had obviously told them that I had been taken away by the police. He also had the video evidence from Connor that watched me throw his clothes out of my bedroom onto the landing. She had also spoken to Connor about me and he obviously reinforced what his dad had been telling him and showing him. Yet another set up how stupid had I been to have not realised what he was actually up to in trying to get my home off me. Anthony was sat on the double sofa in the kitchen and as I glanced at him I thought you pathetic moron he was sat with his head in his hands down in his lap saying "Look what she has done to me and our family" of course blaming me yet again for everything as he always did. He was all dishevelled looking really sorry for himself and obviously trying to get her sympathy. This behaviour is commonly known as being the persuader and they use the children or anybody else for that matter to work in his favour by getting them all on his side with their acting. I told the social worker that this man is not forlorn he runs about a third of the country as a manager in a national service company. He is highly intelligent, cunning and manipulative and dangerous and this is all an act. She just sat there looking at me spread out in the chair. I then said that I want my keys to this house as it was still my home and my name was still on the deeds to the house and it was mine before he came into my life. Anthony said he hadn't got the keys and after some time of me telling the social worker that he would know exactly where they were as he was so fastidious then funnily enough he produced the keys out of his back pocket in front of us both. He then gave me the keys and I said to her "I will leave but I need to get some clothes and toiletries" I then went upstairs after her agreeing it was ok to do so. To my horror when I entered my bedroom there must have been fifty empty bottles on the bed and in the wardrobe including empty beer cans and bottle of spirits. All empty all over the bed so no one could have got in or out of that bed. Yet the police took me out of the bed in my pyjamas and to the police station when there were no bottles on the bed. Otherwise how could I have slept in it? So who put the bottles on the bed for the social worker? Anthony of course as he had been planning and storing them up for some time and now I knew why. That's why the wheelie bin had not been put out. I didn't drink, as already mentioned, spirits, beer, lager or anything else I only drank wine. If you were to see the amount of bottles that were in the bedroom you would have died laughing and if I had drank it all I would have been dead. There was no correlation between the police and social worker. I told her they weren't mine and that the police had got me out of that bed last night and they would have verified to her that there were no bottles on that bed at the time of my departure. So he had stitched me up like a kipper and I fell for it and so did the police, social worker, colleagues, friends and my son. I took what I needed at the time for work and I took a photograph of my son and came downstairs. I got the keys off Anthony who remained silent and I left my home. I never got back in my home ever again not even when he tried to sell it from underneath me by putting it up for sale on a website in his name only full well knowing that I owned half of it and that I wouldn't agree at that time to the sale. I left all my jewellery behind and all my personnel possessions and I have never to this day seen my son again apart from when he was in Urmston with a friend going into the barbers and I recognised his walk but I couldn't go up to him with his friend there as I didn't want to cause any upset and when I saw him once when I had made an appointment to see the social worker to explain my side of the story later on. He was walking along the road with his friend Mark. He saw my car driving past and I looked in my mirror and he was shaking his fists at me which nearly broke my heart. He didn't know about Katherine but he had seen some of the violence towards me but he hadn't really known exactly what was going on he had only been shown what Anthony wanted him to see.

We had a joint bank account and as mentioned he was syphoning his money away and only mine was going in for all the bills, mortgage and essentials, he only topped it up when needed so I left the house with no money at all. However, I saw a credit card on the side when I was leaving so I took it and I knew the pin number but only bought about a hundred pounds worth of essentials that I needed. The social worker left my home with me and I said to her that she had got it all wrong and that I was a victim of domestic violence but she didn't believe me either. Anthony had played such a good part in this he should have got an Oscar. I said to her that she had not even investigated or didn't know that I had been beaten two weeks before and had reported it to the police with a view to prosecuting him. She had not liaised with anyone other than Anthony and Connor.

I returned to my home on the Sunday night after the Saturday having stayed at my mums. I wanted to get the rest of my things out. However, my keys wouldn't fit as he had changed the locks. So the keys he gave me in front of the social worker wouldn't have worked and he knew that then. I then went round to my neighbour's house and phoned the police to say he had locked me out of my home and I needed to collect my things. They advised they would be coming and we waited for over an hour and in the end my neighbour called them again but they just never turned up. I felt that they hadn't believed me on previous occasions so didn't think I was worth turning up for.

The week before I was thrown out of my own home I had arranged to take my daughter and her husband to the theatre where the play Fanny by Gaslight was showing. I explained to them that this was the process of gas lighting and what had been happening to me to make me look mentally ill so that the husband could get away with murder and keep the house and money. Also he would have been really wealthy if I had died of drink as I had a long length of service and I was still employed at that point. I had spoken to my daughter on the phone and asked her not to be late as they won't let you in as it's a live performance. She then received a phone call from Anthony saying that her "mother was drunk out of her head in the house again". Rachel said "well Anthony that's funny as I have just spoken with my mum and she sounds perfectly well to me and we are meeting in half an hour to go to the theatre". I went to the theatre with Rachel who can confirm that I turned up without any alcohol in my system whatsoever. Anthony was even trying to ruin the relationship with my daughter but it failed thank God as he had succeeded with so many others in his plot to destroy me. I told Connor what had happened and his retort to me was that his dad had told him that he was going to get the house because he earned more money than you. Connor also knew that I was completely ok and not drunk. Katherine performed exactly the same as Anthony in my investigation by lying about me, for instance saying that I was attending domestic violence meetings and appointments drunk. That was a complete and utter barefaced lie. I have since gained evidence from the professional bodies that I attended, in writing, that I never attended any meetings drunk or in any way sounded drunk on the phone. The NHS investigation did not carry out any checks on her evidence they just believed it and completely ignored me.

The reason I committed myself to the bedroom in the first place, being terrified of him , was that I had been out with Anne and Edna when Katherine just turned up to the pub in Flixton for what I would call a late lunch. We all worked Thursday mornings so we always used to meet up about 1pm for a girlie lunch. I had continued to go to these as I was trying to have some normality in my life. We all talked about various issues and what we had all been up to. At this point I had a gut feeling that something was amiss with Katherine and had suspicions of her at that time with regards to my husband Anthony. I had no concrete evidence but two and two made five. Also at the lunch I had mentioned to Edna that Anthony and I were having some friends round for dinner on Saturday night and that they were all heavy drinkers. I was concerned about how much it was all going to cost. Edna mentioned that her son sold wine and he had some that I could have for about £2 a bottle. She said if I followed her home I could collect the wine from her son so that's exactly what I did. During the meal we all shared a bottle of wine which was about a glass each. We didn't have anymore because we were all in our cars. We all left and I followed Edna to her son's home and bought a box of wine which only cost me twelve pounds instead of nearly thirty. So I was quite pleased with this and it was solely for the party on Saturday evening. The meal was for six and having only four chairs Anthony and I had gone out the previous Sunday and bought two lovely leather chairs from a furniture shop. So we were both still playing the marriage game even though he was having affairs and abusing me. He could easily play the game of being a good husband and being really pleasant at times but then if it wasn't going his way he turned from Jekyll into Hyde. I got home around three thirty pm on the Thursday afternoon and sat in the kitchen and made myself a coffee. I was sat at the far end of the kitchen with my cookbook and coffee. I was looking at the recipes as I was making the meal on Saturday and I was looking for a really good sauce to go with the fish that I was cooking. I was quite surprised as at four thirty, which was early for him as he didn't finish work until then and would go to play a game of squash first, Anthony walks through the kitchen door. My eyes are down reading the book and at the other end of the kitchen, so he couldn't smell my breath and couldn't tell from my body language that I had a drink at lunchtime and he stormed in shouting at me that I had been drinking. I was scared as I knew what could be coming so I tried to protect myself by saying that I didn't know what he was talking about. I thought to myself how does he know that I had been to lunch and had a glass of wine? *(I thought to myself it's that cow she must have phoned him)*. I got up and quietly walked past him to go to my bedroom. However, he followed me and again was being aggressive and goading me into admitting that I had had a drink. I just ignored him climbed into bed and put the covers over my head and he didn't like that because he wasn't getting the drama which he needed. I was shaking under the bedclothes praying for him not to hit me again and also thinking thank God I had put the divorce papers in with the solicitor. I had started to do something about him and made a decision to leave after having requested help from many sources one was the police. I got no help from the police at all and they didn't even believe me. Eventually he went down stairs to my relief and I gave a big sigh. At that point I made a decision to tell him that I was divorcing him and needed the courage to tell him. So foolishly I went and got one of the bottles of wine that was for the dinner party and drank over the next few hours thinking about how to approach him to tell him I had actually come to a point where I could take no more from him. I was never one for letting go. I went downstairs later that evening and he was in the lounge at the back of the house and was sat there drinking as he usually did he was always drinking. I picked up the courage as I couldn't say anything when I was sober through fear and told him exactly what I was doing and was divorcing him. When I said this I was stood by the lounge door he said I wouldn't even be able to get a solicitor let alone divorce him and on what grounds? I told him that I was divorcing him on domestic violence and told him the solicitors name and said that all his details were already with her. He obviously didn't believe me and then said anyway I have a girlfriend so what do I need you for. I felt absolutely gutted as he had been denying his affairs for years and years. I don't know why I was so gutted by it because I knew really but to have him admit it in such a way was quite painful. We continued to have words about this but then all of a sudden he stopped talking and just sat and eerily stared at me. It was horrible and he looked like the devil. I was, understandably, upset and went on to say that he had tried to destroy me and my family with his behaviour, affairs, abuse, and violence over the years of our marriage and yet had the audacity to blame everything on me. There was an icy stillness in the room almost the lull before the storm and I became really frightened as he left his chair like a dragon and grabbed hold of me and dragged me over the foot stool, out through the lounge door into the hallway, then he had me by the throat, one hand on my throat and one hand on my left arm and he smacked my head so violently against the integral garage door, three times that I can remember, I thought I was going to die. The thoughts swirling around my mind were that this was it he was going to kill me now. The back of my head was so painful and I had a searing burning sensation up my neck through to the top of my head. He just dropped me to the floor like a rag doll. My throat hurt where he had held it so tight I could hardly swallow and my arm was throbbing with his grip as his fingers had stuck in my skin. For a skinny guy he was strong. This was the last violent attack leading up to me leaving and divorcing him. The fact that he threw me out when the social worker was there probably saved my life. I believe if I had of stayed in that relationship and home I would not be here to tell you this story. There were at least four occasions of violence towards me from Anthony where I could have died from the blows or been seriously disabled as the violence was always directed towards my neck and head.

Whenever he lost control and couldn't get what he wanted he then resorted to the violence to keep me in my place which was right under his thumb at all times. The rules of his game were that women are possessions and that I should obey him at all times. He used abusive behaviour to keep his rules in place and when I refused this day to comply with his rules by divorcing him it shattered his belief and he got feelings of panic, powerlessness and outrage because I dared to stand up to him. He then lost control and went for me.

He had often said over the years that I was a bad mother and a slut to most people including my son. The only person who had ever known different and had stood up to him was Laney who I had now lost contact with. He really truly believed it was ok to be violent to hurt me and actually kill me and he used excuses for himself. Occasionally after these attacks in the past he would promise me a present or a meal. So he was trying to re-establish the rules again so I would be subservient to him and he could do what the fuck he liked. He actually said to me one night whilst we were walking home from his friend's house that all I had to do was look after Connor and him and stay in the house and everything would be fine. I thought at the time that he was mad. He wanted me in the home as his little slave whilst he partied with any women that agreed to it and was under his spell. Our little talk whilst walking home was only about three weeks before this attack on me. I knew when he said these things to me that I was in a very dangerous place and I would have to get out. That's exactly what I started to do.

After he dropped me like a rag doll he just went back into the lounge sat down and started drinking I went up to my bedroom. All this time Connor was up in his room. I rang my mum and started to tell her what had just happened but she didn't know what to do she had the early onset of dementia and was a lovely mother and always listening to me. I got through the night and wasn't working the next day. I awoke in the morning to see him getting ready to go to work in my bedroom. He just looked at me coldly, not mentioning what he had done and never saying sorry, and I said to him who is the girlfriend then. He turned to look at me and said I only made that up. He went on to say that he had found my stash of wine to which I advised him it wasn't mine I had bought it for Saturday evening as it was a cheap deal. He wasn't accepting any of my explanations and went off to work after slagging me off the whole time he was getting ready. I was so traumatised by these recent events with no apology for smacking my head and was quite confused at this time. I thought he had loved me but I hadn't realised he was a sociopath at the time we met and it hadn't really surfaced. When he told me he had a girlfriend he actually broke my heart having given my time and love to him for all those years and looking after our son. I decided to go out and I bought a bottle of wine took it back home like a trophy and I drank a couple of glasses to pluck up the courage to ring the police although I had very little faith in them I felt I would not be able to prosecute Anthony without giving some kind of statement. A police officer arrived and took my statement he was only a young man and I do appreciate that I may have come across as quite incoherent to him as I was exhausted, upset, confused, and traumatised by my life with Anthony. Whatever I was feeling and however I came across to the police officer with my hand on my heart I was telling the truth about everything. The officer went away and probably thought I was a raving nutter. I didn't hear anything else until I heard that they had arrested Anthony at the Health Club when he had picked Connor up and took him to the Health Club with him. I only knew this because Katherine phoned me to tell me. She also went on to say to me that getting Anthony arrested at the Health Club would only culminate in the end of my marriage to him. I don't have a clue how she knew as she didn't say so she could have been there with him at the time. Connor would not have thought it unusual for Anthony and Katherine to be together as she had been my friend. I don't think I replied to Katherine when she told me but I do remember thinking what the fuck has it got to do with you anyway. What I do or say about my marriage or within it had nothing to do with her. I only presume Anthony had Connor taken to his friend Mark's house for the weekend. I never saw Connor after that as Anthony had already set me up with Mark's mum that I was an unfit mother, etc. On the Saturday I had a phone call from the police saying there was insufficient evidence to prosecute so they were letting him out to come home. I couldn't believe it yet again, no one believed me, and I wasn't asked any further questions. I had some bruising on my arm and could feel the bump on my head but the police didn't look at that and they said the bruising was not enough to warrant prosecution. This is what has happened to so many women and their husbands/partners have been let out and then they end up dead.

Anne came to see me a few days after this and she was quite supportive at that time and took some photos of the bruising on my arm. She wouldn't have visited if Anthony was there as she was terrified of him. That's why on many occasions I struggled with the fact that Katherine my so called friend would have wanted him after all she knew and the involvement she had had in bringing me down. I would put my hand on the bible and swear this is the truth. From then on I kept out of his way in, my usual habitat, my bedroom. I ate there, slept there, and showered there and I only went down for a coffee if I knew he wasn't there. I should have just left really but I wanted to keep my house and see my son as I loved him so very much and all this was killing me inside as I could see the gap widening between us.

About a few weeks before all this happened, Anthony had started making casseroles. He prepared them the night before from the slow cooker he had been out and bought. He told people I couldn't cope anymore so had started to do this which meant that Connor could eat at five pm when he wanted to and it meant Anthony didn't have to come home. It still looked like Anthony was being a fantastic dad to everyone but actually he wasn't coming home. He didn't stay out the whole night as he always came home at some point. All this was happening around me but even Connor didn't speak to me at all. I got to the point that I didn't even want anything that Anthony had touched so when I got home from work I would eat egg on toast and then straight up to my room, leaving before him in the morning. After about a week he cottoned on to what I was doing and he was missing out on the abuse he used to give me in the mornings whilst he was getting ready for work. I still managed to get to work. My life at that point was getting up early, getting to work, getting through the day and at this point I had started to mention to my support worker in the car that I thought it was Katherine that was having an affair with Anthony. My support worker was friends with the occupational therapist and Katherine. They all used to go out together socially. I know this because I had been out with them myself. My support worker tried to dissuade me from the thought that it was Katherine as he didn't think it would be her as she had told him in the past that she didn't actually like Anthony. I stopped mentioning anything to him or anyone else again. However, Katherine had also said she didn't like her brother in law but she had an affair with him too. She told me once that she loved athletic men and her brother in law used to run marathons. Her on and off boyfriend played tennis a lot and Anthony played squash every single night at the same health club. My friends at work persuaded me that Katherine wouldn't do that to a friend but they didn't know about her with her twin's husband Stuart or about her other affair with her friend Bernie's husband Luke. Bernie had a knee replacement and Katherine used to go to her home and do some private physiotherapy. Whilst she was there her husband was in the home at the same time. He would be away on the rigs for lengthy times but would have breaks at home for about six weeks. Katherine actually told me herself that whilst Bernie was downstairs she was upstairs on the premise of going to the toilet but was actually kissing and cuddling Bernie's hubby Luke. She also told me that Luke had said he wanted a year out of his marriage to be with Katherine for a while as he didn't want to lose his marriage or his home and money. I told her at the time that he was probably just flirting with her for fun and to leave well alone. She had been seen kissing and cuddling with Luke in swimsuits by her husband at the time. However, I only learnt this part of it when I went to get some help from Dennis many years later. Dennis also told me about the affair with Stuart her brother in law. He said that Stuart was doing jobs around the house for her and making her breakfast early in the morning. This is why Katherine and Dennis got divorced because of the affair with Bernie's husband Luke. Bernie was also his childhood friend since the age of eight and in the end he lost both of them. Bernie and Luke lived in an expensive home in the local area and he worked on the oil rigs and was a big earner. Katherine was interested in men with money and a wealthy image but tired of them quickly so basically was having one affair after the other whether she was married or not at the time. All the men in her life had money and expensive houses.

Returning to my home life, Anthony was making a lot of noise usually on a Saturday morning by throwing bottles in the bin so everyone could hear him. They were his bottles not mine as I was in the bedroom and was hardly drinking at that point. He would fill my bedroom with empty bottles and hide them in the wardrobe. They weren't mine because I wasn't even there and I only ever drank wine. These were cans of beers which he had been noisily throwing in the bin and collecting them as he didn't put the bottle bin out for emptying. Then the sneaky bastard would put them all on my bed and hide in the wardrobe as said and show Connor my son and Charlene his daughter what I had been doing all week in the bedroom. He was planning to get rid of me and although I may have had some drink I would have been dead if I had drank the contents of the cans and bottles. I tried hard to explain to Connor and Charlene that I hadn't even been there and they weren't there when I had left for my mums on Friday evening and that I didn't drink beer. He deliberately planted them in my bedroom to undermine me in front of my son and his daughter. I was becoming very distressed as I could understand why they believed him as there had been previous times when I had been drunk because of the abuse it was the way in which I tried to cope and hide from it all but it served me badly. I believe the picture that he was deliberately painting, to everyone he could, was only part of the truth and he was exaggerating each event out of all proportion to demonstrate to them what he wanted them to believe about me. He wanted me to be without friends, family and children to support me. He also wanted me without any money, reputation, job, so that I would be one hundred per cent reliant upon him. He was extremely manipulative and intelligent; a very clever man. I remember when we were having a barbecue in the garden and there was just Anthony and myself eating and enjoying the sunshine he came up close to my face and in a kind of whispered voice said "Tyff I am the only person who can look after you". This didn't feel like a compliment to me I felt very uncomfortable with that statement it somewhat frightened me. When I tried to break away at the very end of our relationship I was tucked up under the duvet hiding from him when he entered the room I got shivers all over my body and he came really close right up to my face like a slithering snake and said "I am going to make you suffer" those were his exact words. I thought to myself my God don't you think you've made me suffer enough already. I cringed shrinking into the mattress and curling up more into the foetal position. He did make me suffer because for the time being I have lost my son to his control.

There was a really negative energy surrounding my relationship with Katherine. I was foolish to trust her but believed she was my friend. Actually she is no one's friend she just manipulates her way into people's lives on the premise of being their friend. The destruction is often catastrophic for the victims she leaves behind. She has the ability to get under a man's skin and worm her way in, often being friends with the wife and visiting on the premise of this friendship. All the time however she is planning and manipulating her next victim; to try to rob the husband from their wife. Poor blokes don't even see it coming. However, in my husband's case he used to flatter her and she did admit in evidence that he did play mind games with her and flirted with her. She said he often complimented her on her ability to play tennis and on her looks. I wondered why she had not told me at the time but she hid this from me I believe she only admitted this to avoid the confrontation of her having a full blown affair with Anthony, a little bit like The Secret if you've watched the TV series of it, they both planned for my demise and orchestrated all events. They both drank heavily and always in my company yet criticised me for drinking and made massive issues of it and used this as an excuse for the abuse and violence that I was subjected to by both of them. She didn't actually hit me but encouraged me to drink and when I played right into her hands as always, as mentioned earlier, Katherine would go to the toilet and make a call. I am now positive it was to Anthony because he always knew where I was, who I was with, and what I had had to drink. Even if it was only one glass of wine he would still know the exact amount. The only way he could have known this was to put a private detective on me which he did at one point however he could not have afforded this on a long term basis. So he used Katherine and his friend Jason from the health club, a crook from Liverpool, to tell him when and where I was and what I was up to at all times. This is the only rational explanation, unless he is psychic which he isn't, that I can accept. He would have needed all this information to plan my demise. I couldn't see it whilst I was in it but it is so clear to me now and I have spent many moments analysing all the events that took place and I can see how he easily manipulated me and all the others too. He had a very strong personality, a business man, BMW on the drive, lovely home, but superficial charm. He wrapped the police officers and social worker around his little finger almost like the devil. They were just tools in his game to manipulate against me using them against me. So when I went for help to the police he managed to successfully manipulate them and turn them against me. He literally got away with murder and if I hadn't got away from him when I did he would have killed me and most likely got away with it.

Did you know that in the UK a woman is killed by a violent partner every three days and there are very few refuges that woman can go. This was mentioned in a book I obtained and read to help myself understand his behaviour and living with a dominator and the tactics that they use. Considering the statistics that one in four women, maybe more now, will experience domestic violence in their lifetime. The author of the Liberty Programme which is available across venues throughout the UK was a probation officer and worked with hundreds of violent men, some had committed murder. She states that she believed that with her experience spanning many years she thought she had some understanding about domestic violence but she goes on further to state in her book that she later admits she was wrong. She states to her horror that she recognised that she had unwittingly colluded with every abusive man she had ever met. If you are in a violent relationship then please do yourself a big favour and get out and get help from the Liberty Programme. She states in her book and this resonated right through my very being when I read these words:

"A women/man who has been abused has some understanding of what has happened to her. This is simply not true when a woman is being subjected to abuse she feels that she is in the middle of a very confusing mess and that it must be somehow his or her fault".

This is why the author started the Liberty Programme. She ran it initially for women who were on probation for committing offences that she can now see were the result of being subjected to abuse.

I actually did the same at one point because I was so frustrated that Anthony would not let me have anything out of my own house, e.g. no photos of my children growing up, none of my own jewellery, no personal items at all, my crystal glass collection, my coin collection which I had collected as a child, and even my mobile phone. He even wouldn't let me have my birth certificate. You can imagine how difficult for me this was. Basically I went to my home one day travelling by bus as I had had a drink and I knocked on the door and no one was in. I was so frustrated and angry that I walked to the local shops and bought some eggs and I bet you can guess what I did with them, yes, I threw them all over the front of my house. I should not have wasted my money and should have made an omelette out of them which would have been more beneficial for me. I went around the back of the house and I sat on my wedding plant, I can't type for laughing, and ripped it to shreds. I then tipped over the patio furniture which was mine after all and then I threw some pots around. I think I am making light of this but actually I destroyed the back garden. I threw a pot at the back patio window thinking to myself it's my pot and my window. However, Mr Plod didn't see my point of view. One of my neighbours came out and asked if I was alright and I said to her "Yes I feel fucking great throwing eggs at my own house as that bastard deserves payment for beating me up for years. The interesting fact is that the police must have been called and they spoke to Maggie and she told them that she had seen me throwing eggs at the house but that this woman has been to my house distressed and had told me that her husband had been hitting her and also that the house belonged to Tyff before Anthony arrived on the scene. The police decided not to take a statement from her and didn't want to know this Maggie told me this later on. They went to other neighbours houses and finally got a statement from one of them which fitted their way of getting a conviction. The police arrived at my new little home in Flixton at around 4am and they took me in a police van in handcuffs again and I was taken to the police hotel for an overnight stay. It's a rubbish hotel and the menu is crap. I never want to stay there again. I was taken to court with a free solicitor and I gave all the evidence to her of all the abuse that I had suffered throughout my marriage and that went in front of two male judges who decided to give me an eighteen -month restraining order and a criminal record which remains with me now. I was actually given the opportunity to speak to the two judges as to why I had behaved in such a manner. I went on to explain to them in depth the domestic violence and abuse that I had suffered for many years. Their answer to me was, wait for it, irrelevant and that I should be able to keep control of my actions. In other words they didn't give a flying fuck that I had been subjected to a life of severe violence and abuse and how that affects the victim's behaviour. Once again Anthony had won and I was the one that looked like a complete nut job. I probably was a little bit at that time. Well not a nut job basically abused and very angry that he kept getting away with it and that no one ever believed me. I feel that the justice system protected him.

I could no longer go to my home or even down Roxford Avenue. I was not allowed there at all and would have been arrested and could have gone to jail. When I arrived at my mums house with no belongings my brother intervened and left Anthony a message on his phone that I required my clothes and personal items and that he wanted them. Several weeks later Anthony arranged to bring my clothes and he delivered a couple of old suitcases (the crappy ones that he wouldn't want) full of my clothes just shoved in any old way and the rest were in bin bags. Eight big bags in total and I messaged him to ask where all my jewellery was. He text back saying they might be in one of the bags so you better look for it. He didn't say the jewellery was there or not only that I had better look for it. He text me several times, once to say it was such a shame that Jack, the neighbour opposite had passed away, and also another neighbour who we didn't really know or like had passed away which I thought was quite bizarre of him. So I text back that life can be very sad at times. He sent another text some days later to say that he had a couple of really nice cardigans and would he like me to bring them over. Again most bizarre, but being nice to me was his way of getting back in control. I just text him back saying that I didn't want them or for him to come near me. On another occasion a male friend who went to the same dance club as me invited me for a coffee so I agreed and we went to the Treeford Centre, somebody must have seen me with my friend and phoned Anthony and subsequently I received yet another text saying "Who was the unlucky man". I didn't respond. The final text was about the credit card that I had taken with me, after all it was joint, and I bought a hundred pounds' worth of bits and pieces from the local furniture store for my new home when I found it. He said that he had cancelled the card and it was basically theft. I never responded.

When I was living at my mum's I received a phone call from the Health Club stating that my husband had been in and cancelled my membership which I had always paid for myself out of my salary. This was his way of saying that he wasn't allowing me to go to the Health Club now and I was really annoyed with the Health Club. He was systematically destroying everything and everyone that meant anything to me. I had to go into the Health Club and set up a new membership. After that appointment which was very upsetting for me I then went to the wholesalers and cancelled his membership from my card. I thought at the time two can play at that game. This unfortunately instigated yet a further text as he had gone, says me laughing, to the wholesale warehouse to get the shopping and he had gone to the till and put it all on the belt and his card had been rejected. He was told he was not a member anymore and of course he couldn't just get an account like that it would have had to be through his workplace. The text this time was very angry saying he was only buying the shopping for our son, who of course hated me by now, so I text him back advising him it was a bit like him cancelling my Health Club membership, and I also said what he always had said to me "Tough, shit happens". I felt really ly empowered by doing to him what he had done to me and he didn't like it one little bit.

By now the divorce was in progress but very slow as he wouldn't agree to anything. I was putting domestic violence into the petition. The travelling was getting me down as I was travelling from Marple Bridge to my job at the Health Centre daily and the traffic was horrific and my manager did accommodate me by increasing my hours on a Thursday. They would not allow me to reduce my hours still having to do ten am to four pm Monday, Tuesday, Wednesday and Thursday morning now. My solicitor was in Urmston only twenty minutes from my workplace so I had to make up the time spent there. Most of the information needed was actually back at my home.

I left my home in November as previously mentioned and I was struggling to get to work and function as a human being at that time. None of my so called friends visited me at my mum's house. Not one of them came to see me. However, Katherine needed to know what was going on so I got texts requesting information from her and she asked to meet up with me at the Mersey Pub in Sale on a Thursday afternoon. We both met up after work. I accepted her offer as I was feeling very down and low and needed someone to talk to. More fool me I should have known better with all the experiences I had with her. However, I was finding it difficult to cut her off as a friend after our relationship of nearly twenty years. I arrived at the pub about 1pm and Katherine was forty five minutes late. I was waiting so as she got out of her car I walked over to her. I immediately mentioned that I didn't have a lot of time as I had an appointment with the women's charity that were helping me have protection in the form of panic alarms, fire proof letterbox and smoke alarms as they were treating the situation as a serious risk to me and my mum. Katherine said "Ok no worries we will just have a quick coffee". I said yes that's fine. We both made our way to the bar and Katherine offered to get me a drink adding that she felt I seemed really very stressed and that I needed a glass of wine. I have to admit I was really stressed and was an idiot to agree and accepted her offer. We were chatting about this and that of my events and she was talking about her divorce situation. I also mentioned that I would have to look for another house.

Neither of us should have been drinking alcohol really as we were both still in our uniforms although off duty. At this time I felt quite secure in her company and we chatted for nearly forty five minutes until I mentioned that it was the time for me to leave to go to my appointment. Katherine was very persuasive and encouraged me to stay and was quite insistent about this. As I was very vulnerable at the time I told her I would just phone and rearrange my appointment. I returned to the table to continue chatting with her after the call. She said to me that she would get me another drink. She was waving her credit card in her hand back and forth whilst saying to me that as long as there was money on her card she would always get me a drink. She was positively encouraging me to drink.

Whilst chatting about my thoughts of buying a new home she mentioned she was struggling with her mortgage and if that she wasn't very careful she may lose her home and she really needed to meet a rich man to help her out. I remember very clearly her saying this to me. Interestingly, she got me the glass of wine but got herself a coffee and yet she could drink for England and very often did. I now started to feel a bit nervous at this point and my gut instinct kicked in. I felt apprehensive and wondered to myself what game was she playing now. I sipped the second glass of wine really slowly but to reassure her that I was actually drinking it. Katherine then got up and said she was going to the loo. (As previously mentioned Katherine always goes to the loo to use her phone). She was gone for quite a while and eventually came back and sat down with me again.

Some fifteen minutes later a tall dark haired man, in his fifties, walked into our area of the pub with a large glass of red wine in his hand. He made his way over to the table opposite, but so as to face us. He smiled and said "Hello girls" and then sat himself down. He then made a phone call and he was speaking quite loud as if he wanted us to hear but he was speaking in Italian and I don't understand a word of that language. During the conversation he turned to us and said "Huh women". After the phone call he began to chat to us from across the room saying that he was staying at the Cresta in Altrincham. He went on to tell us that he was doing a presentation the next day in Manchester and he was asking whether it would be cheaper to go by tram or drive in and pay the parking fees. I said that I didn't know because I didn't live in Altrincham and didn't drive into Manchester. He then added that he was on his way back from a visit to Urmston, as he was thinking of moving back there, and had called in to the pub on his way through to the Cresta in Altrincham. I was quite suspicious hearing this as I thought to myself why call in to a pub on your way to have drinks when you could drive ten minutes more to your hotel and have as much as you like and not have to get back into a car. The basic chit chat continued and he was becoming quite cheeky with his comments and a nuisance really. He said to us that we were a pair of cats and not kittens. His innuendo was quite pathetic and it wasn't real. He didn't seem to be a stupid man who would make such a comment. The chit chat was broken by Katherine getting up to go to the loo again. He then gets up out of his seat, walks over to our table, and sits down next to me. I thought to myself OMG I just wanted him to disappear. I was trying to have a conversation with my friend not some idiot in a bar who was acting strangely.

Katherine returned from the loo and sits opposite him and he then offers to get us all another drink. Katherine quickly said "No thanks" but I said I would just have a small one just to placate him and he returned with a very large glass of red wine for me. I had no intention of drinking it.

In Katherine's statement to the internal investigation team at work she stated that the man had bought me two large glasses of red wine but this was a lie. A further ten minutes passed with me listening to his innate patter and suddenly Katherine got up and said she was leaving but didn't ask if I was going with her. In hindsight I should have said at that point that I was leaving also. However, I managed to change the topic from his pathetic chat up lines to cars. There was actually method in my madness as I wanted to find out what car he was driving because. I then got up on the premise of going to the loo so I could have a look outside to see if the vehicle he mentioned was out there. It was and it was also a very expensive large white vehicle. He told me it was from his company's fleet of cars. He said he had come from Italy to do this presentation in Manchester but just happened to go to Urmston as he used to live there. I then couldn't believe that he would be worrying about car park fees. I returned from the loo and could have kicked myself as stupidly I had left my phone on the table. He had the number that was written on the back. This was down to Anthony insisting that he put this on my phone so I knew the number as it was my works phone.

I eventually left the man saying I was going to visit my friends and astonishingly he actually wanted to come with me. I told him straight that he couldn't. Instead of going straight to my car I walked up the road for about twenty minutes to give him time to leave as I did not trust him at all. I then went back to the pub and searched around to make sure that he and his car had gone. I went back into the pub myself and ordered some coffee and sat there for an hour or so to make sure that the alcohol was mostly out of my system. I then went back to my car and made my way home.

I didn't have any contact with Katherine from the time she left the pub, however, she told the investigating officers at work that she did ring me and that when I answered I was very drunk on the phone. This is a lie.

My journey home was about forty minutes or so and if Katherine was such a good friend, as she was always saying, why did she not come back to make sure I was safe. She left me with a man neither of us knew stating that I was extremely drunk. Not such a good friend after all?

On my way home I received a call on my mobile and I parked up and answered the phone and alarmingly it was the man from the pub asking me how my driving was going. I thought go away you stupid man. I told him that I was fine and that I would not be meeting up with him as he wanted but to please inform Katherine and Anthony that I was aware that he was a set up and it wasn't very bright of them. Of course, he denied this so I just hung up on him. It was all so strange and too coincidental and nothing added up. I sat in the car thinking that they had paid him to set me up. I also thought I wonder how long it would take for them to contact him to tell them what I had said to him. It was only five minutes later that my worst fears were realised when she sent a text to find out if I was OK. This was three hours after she had left me in the pub. I was so gutted I didn't respond to her text. This was yet another one of her set ups to get me in trouble.

I arrived home feeling down and despondent having realised what had just happened and had some dinner and relaxed. However, in Katherine's statement she had put that she had called me when I arrived home and that I was fine. This didn't happen. Amazing how you can be as drunk as a skunk, drive home safely, and then be fine as Katherine stated.

Later that evening I made the decision to call her and I told her that I thought she and Anthony were setting me up. She defended herself and Anthony saying that I made up everything about Anthony and none of it was true. She then went on to say I was a terrible mother to Connor and that he deserved better than me. Also that Anthony had not loved me for years. This escalated into a massive row over the phone with her completely agreeing with everything that Anthony had ever done. She knew that I was being abused as she was in the hallway when he punched me in the face and showed no remorse at all.

In all her statements she turned everything around to use against me and the phone call was going nowhere so I hung up on her.

The following day I received a phone call from Anne and even she was now annoyed with me as Katherine had obviously been on the phone to her and told her everything. Again trying to cause issues between me and Anne. Anne asked me how I could believe that Katherine her twin sister had set me up. I knew that Anne's husband Stuart had been having a long affair with Katherine but Anne didn't know that I knew of it. Katherine had told me all about the affair herself. I would never have mentioned this to Anne as I had no intention of ever hurting her. I did back down eventually on the phone with Anne as I did not want to lose her as my friend as I had known her for thirty years.

Whilst I was staying at my mum's house the only person who came to see me was a lady called Sarah Clarke who was a work colleague but had been to her house and we both had children at the same age. She brought with her a beautiful bouquet of flowers and I was very touched by her visit. I had arranged to go on a tennis holiday with Katherine, Edna and Jane Heathfield which had been booked some six months prior to the problems. When I realised I couldn't go on that holiday I had information about where we were staying and I telephoned to discuss. To my amazement Katherine had already cancelled the week and booked a prior week for herself, Edna and Jane Heathfield yet no one had the decency to let me know. That told me everything I needed to know about these so called friends.

# CHAPTER 5

# The Finance Plot

Anthony had started his finance plot by having all of his money transferred into a separate account in his name. I was told that all my money should be kept in the joint account for such as the mortgage, household bills, food, his motorbike monthly payment of three hundred and eighty five pounds per month and anything else that I needed. He told me that he would top this up on a monthly basis if it was necessary. He told me that he may change this if and when he felt I was behaving myself and agreeing to his demands and went on to say that it was all my fault that I had hurt myself and nearly died and nothing to do with him. He felt I had been irresponsible by falling out of the window, from the top floor, whilst escaping from him so he now had to take control of the money pot. Looking back I had an inheritance of about four thousand pounds when my dear old dad died and Anthony used most of that money for his own needs such as motorbike stuff. I had actually said that I wanted to get a cabinet to remember him by and place his photo on top. I never got this as it was denied me by Anthony. My son Connor also received two thousand pounds from my dad and my daughter received the same. She actually got her money and I do believe Connor did not have that money he did buy him a bike which was worth three hundred and five pounds so that was probably the sum total of what my son received from my dad.

He still had a very exuberant lifestyle going on holidays with his daughter and friends and I was never invited. He did allow me to look after Connor which was strange considering he was telling everyone I was such an unfit mother. He was spending a lot of money on himself and his daughter now. I actually said I would have liked to have flown out to Austria with his friend's wife as she had a bad back and was not able to travel on the motorbike. I had even managed for Connor to be looked after. However, he refused as he didn't want to pay the money for the flight. He was now taking control of all the money and restricting me from going anywhere. The holidays of his always coincided with our anniversary or my birthday so I was always left on my own.

I was not drinking anymore and was able to drive everywhere and I was treated like the chauffeur by Anthony. As his daughter Charlene was more and more on the scene and was treated like his best friend, as she of course loved the motorbike, taking her to the pub whilst leaving me at home and I was at that time trying to pay off the twenty five grand that we were in debt due to the holiday in Australia, the motorbike, and the six thousand pound balloon payment for the motorbike. I had thought that the motorbike was on a straight forward finance agreement. However, it wasn't that type of agreement and there was a balloon payment. At this point I knew I needed some money of my own in case of an emergency and I called it my Running Away Pot. I went to the bank and asked to have a private discussion and to have this witnessed by a second person from the bank as I needed to open another account and I specified this must be private and confidential. This was arranged and I spoke in a private room for at least forty minutes and this account was to be in my name only and the address of my mum's house. I stressed that I was a victim of abuse and I did not want any statements to be sent to my home address. I opened this account with about ten pounds in it and added small amounts regularly. I only had about thirty in the account and I arrived home one day and Anthony had opened some mail addressed to him welcoming him to his new account. I nearly had a fit and couldn't believe how incompetent the bank could be. Why they wrote to him I will never know. I was then left in the hot seat to quickly come up with an excuse for why I had done this before I had been annihilated by the University Challenge champ. I light heartedly said "Oh you have spoilt my surprise, I was putting it away for a special present for your birthday" this was a load of shit really but he actually swallowed it because it was only a small amount and it fed his ego. You will understand how angry I was with the bank of who I am no longer with and I put a complaint in and was really angry on the phone. They put twenty pounds compensation in I ask you when I could have lost my teeth over that one. I couldn't be bothered to fight anymore. I then started to put money in the house instead in a little black bag and I had reached one hundred and fifty pounds and I came home one day and he had emptied every draw there was in the bedroom and had found my money stash. I remember telling Katherine all about this and telling her I was going to have to keep it in my bedroom and hide it. So you will understand when I say that the sneaky bitch must have told him how else would he have known that and why would he search the bedroom. Why I kept telling her anything is beyond me now. I did not believe that someone could be that evil and had trusted her. He took my money stash and this is when he started the money list in the kitchen. I was ordered to write every single penny that I had spent down on this piece of paper oh and the date. He actually put his down too i.e. the Berkshire Pub – 2 pints etc. He used the excuse of us running out of money to do this but don't forget he had his own stash and of course I wasn't allowed to talk about or mention it so basically he was living off me and I paid the mortgage for the last twelve months of our relationship and the motorbike. Anthony was earning about fifty five thousand pounds per annum plus his company vehicle and had a large pension pot. So he was really well off and not using any of it for us. His money pot was like a honey pot to Katherine and she buzzed around him like a queen bee as she was quite a lazy person so I can't call her a worker bee. That's all she could see the money plot was her game.

When I was living at my mum's my petrol bill was enormous because of me driving from Marple Bridge to Partington every day. I had called into the garage to fuel up and my card was refused. I was lucky as I had some cash on me so I was able to pay for it and leave the garage. I phoned the bank the next day and he had closed our joint account. He now made it impossible for me to get my own money and I had just worked a full month and my pay had gone in to the bank of one thousand six hundred and fifty pounds which he was now going to keep. He was quite happy to take my last wage and leave me with no money at all, to even get to work. I therefore had to borrow money from my mum. For once in my life luck was on my side as he had closed it knowing that my money would go in. However, he wasn't as clever as he thought on this occasion as my money hit the account on the midnight hour of the day he had closed it. So the money bounced out as the account was closed. Thank God I had thought and I then chased my money to find out where it had gone. So I opened a new account for the company to put my salary in. I then had my own account now. He was the type of man that would have taken your last sweet out of your packet. Another attempt to cause me anxiety and stress and as much damage as he could. He was a real conman, a liar, a thief and abuser.

Within a week of me moving in with my mum I was of course really traumatised by what had happened. I then received a call from the Child Support Agency who spoke to me advising me that I was the deserting parent. I told them that I was not allowed back in to my own home and that I had not left voluntarily and that my husband was abusive. I also told them that of course I would pay maintenance for my son but I had not actually had any time to discuss this with my husband. I asked for them to confirm this in writing to me what was expected and when. This happened within days of me being removed from my home. I told them to send me a letter about it. This reared its ugly head later on in the divorce settlement where my husband stated that I had never paid any maintenance even though the CSA were involved and I had been paying every month by direct debit to the CSA who then paid him. I had to get a statement from the CSA to prove in court that I had always paid, so yet again he was lying about me. I think he was falling to bits at this point as he was making obvious mistakes. The CSA then sent the proof of maintenance payments to my husband's solicitor and on their communication to his solicitors they had put my new address on it. This new address is really relevant as to how Katherine's twin Anne found my house and came to visit about sixteen months after I had bought it. Even if she had driven around the area she couldn't have known or found out where I lived as I didn't have a car at that time either. The only way that she could have found out my new address was through Anthony by way of his solicitor. He must have told Katherine who then told Anne. On 20th January 2013 I was sent home from work whilst they carried out an investigation into my behaviour and I did not speak to either of the twins from the 25th January and did not buy my new house until the end of May 2013. I had told people I had seen some houses and was thinking of buying one but had not indicated to anyone about one in particular. So Anne turned up at my house she was really chatty asking me how I was (I actually think she was on a fact finding mission for Katherine) and what was I doing and what was I up to. I remember telling her that I had had a nervous breakdown and we just chatted about life in general. This was three and a half years ago and before the court cases held in London. I mentioned that I had seen Katherine at the bus stop and she had got out of her car to come and talk to me. I spoke to her and asked how her twin Anne was and how Jane Heathfield was and that I missed Anne. Anne told me that at that time Katherine was going back out with Matt Harding and I didn't say anything to her about what I knew.

The final insult came to me after having bought my new home with money loaned from my brother. I was paying him back by way of a set amount monthly until the sale of our home however, I found out through a friend of mine, Della Windel, by text that my house was for sale on a website. I then looked at the website and saw my house for sale which made me really angry and I thought to myself you cheeky lowlife bastard. Although, there was a restraining order against me I went to the top of the cul de sac and I could clearly see the for sale sign outside my house. This was news to me. I went along to the estate agent who was selling our home and I asked to view it. She stated what a lovely home it was and there had been a lot of interest and that Anthony would be happy to show me around at any time and when would I like to view. I was choking back the laughter and I said to her that I really didn't think he would like to show me around. She said no not at all he is really desperate to sell quickly and at that point in the conversation I nearly wet myself. Trying to contain myself from the laughter I said again that it wouldn't be a good idea as I am Anthony's wife and I am divorcing him and only just saw my house for sale on your website without my permission. She said "Oh no, no, Mr Montisford is the sole owner of that property and everything is above board". I said "Well that's very strange as it is still half my house and my name is very clearly on the deeds. If you would like to speak with my solicitor she is only around the corner from you". I then went on to tell her that my soon to be ex-husband is a conman and if you do not remove the property from the market immediately I will have you reported. I would advise you to send Anthony Montisford a letter requesting some form of reimbursement for wasting your time and lying to you. She was really shocked and went to speak to the manager and they asked me to go into his office where they spoke with me again about what I had said. I told him to contact my solicitor for proof. They promptly took the house off the market. They obviously contacted my solicitor and Anthony. I tried to tell the police but they weren't interested as it wasn't actually fraud because I had stopped it. However, I believe it was fraud as he had lied to the estate agents and tried to sell the house from underneath me hence the very quick sale he wanted. He actually could have got away with this as he had my birth certificate and would never return it. I could only have thought that on a serious note if he had of sold the house without my consent and my name being on the deeds he would have had to have someone playing me with my birth certificate as proof. Also he would have had my name on some household bills which he could have used and said that I didn't have a passport and couldn't drive as I was banned. He could have easily got away with three hundred thousand pounds which was the value of our house and what it eventually sold for. He tried to dirty my name even further in the divorce proceedings stating that I had turned up at the estate agents and caused a massive scene of which then I had to get a letter from the estate agents. More stupid mistakes on his part he really was getting very desperate now. They wrote back confirming that I was extremely dignified in my approach with them. So you can see the lies he was making up trying to destroy me in every way he could. Katherine had done exactly the same in the investigation at work by saying that I had turned up to the domestic violence meetings drunk. I then provided evidence of this lie and the domestic violence team have put this in writing. Also I mentioned that the NHS had never checked with the Domestic Violence Team or contacted them in any manner to check if Katherine's version in her signed statement was actually the truth. If they had of checked they would have realised that she was lying too. I have the letter from TDAS dated 10th May 2016 and it actually states that Mrs Tyff Montisford contacted TDAS in June 2012 in search of information and advice and has received support intermittently thus far. I wish to state that I have never suspected nor had concerns that Mrs Montisford was inebriated during our telephone conversations and appointments. I also wish to assert that I have never been contacted by anyone in a professional capacity from the NHS. This was signed by a Domestic Abuse Advisor. I never saw anyone else other than my doctor and the fellowship and I also attended the Liberty Programme for eleven of the twelve weeks course. They can also vouch that I did not turn up drunk for any of those appointments. Now this is from a woman who is an Professional Body Registrant, and the standards of conduct, performance and ethics state you as such a person holding such a title of responsibility must be honest and trustworthy and this is in the their policy which they wrote. Basically to be a physiotherapist in the NHS you must follow the guidelines set out by the Professional Body as fitness to practice. I have proved myself that Katherine lied in an investigation against me. I feel that they thought I was so ill by now that the two of them Katherine and Anthony could walk away into the shadows with what she thought would be a future with him and all the money from the house, my death in service policy, my pension pot, and his salary. They plotted all this time together to obtain the money and I truly believe that they wanted me to kill myself by drinking. I actually told the Professional Body that I wanted it to be put on record that Anthony and Katherine had conspired together so that I would drink myself to death and they could walk away with all the money.

If I had died they would have got away with it and I feel I am very lucky to be alive. Anthony from this point on never ever gave me a penny with the exception of the four hundred pounds which was left in the joint account. He was quite adamant that I wasn't having any of it but the bank decided it was 50–50 so I was given two hundred pounds in cash that day at the bank and they closed the account. This was now the conclusion of his finance plot and I felt he had to sell the house as he knew that I was back on top, wasn't drinking and had realised his game plan.

# CHAPTER 6

# The Last Nail in my Coffin

The last few months of me living in my home with Anthony and Connor were spent living between my mum's house and my bedroom. I was eating out of tuna cans and various other processed food so I didn't have to see Anthony or be near him. If this sounds quite dramatic to you it's because it truly was a dramatic time in my life. I was absolutely shit scared of him. Around the end of October 2012 I had realised he was seeing another woman who went to the same health club and I also as mentioned suspected Katherine. I was now devastated and occasionally I drank and particularly this specific weekend as I had found out more details about him. This was when he was extremely intimidating and he would stand over me in bed and put his face right into mine saying "I am gonna make you suffer", "You're an alcoholic", "You're an unfit mother", the fact that he drank like a fish didn't seem to be relevant at all. I was guilty this weekend as I drank trying to block the whole thing out of my mind. I got up on the Monday morning and I drove to Shirley Ascot's house and she let me in and I told her that I felt very unwell and had been traumatised by my husband's violence towards me and I needed to talk to her. I was trying to reach out to someone and not really knowing how to do that for the best. She listened to what I had to say and then telephoned our support worker and he said it might be wise for Tyff to go home for the day and ring in sick. So that's exactly what I did. The reason I mention this to you is that Anthony reported me to the Professional Body independently himself stating that I had gone to a colleague's house drunk and asked her for a lift to work. He put that down in writing mentioning the date, which he also got wrong, as he named her incorrectly too. It was a different colleague entirely. I mention this because the two members of staff involved in this with me did not know Anthony professionally, socially or personally. So you might wonder, as I did, how Anthony got this information about me as I didn't tell him and he didn't know them but Shirley was very friendly with my friend and colleague Katherine. Shirley and Katherine were friends and colleagues and this is the only link that I can think of that would and could explain how he knew about this situation. Katherine, Shirley and Stuart Cox, the support worker, were friends outside of work and went out socially together. I had at one time gone out with them socially, very early on, and we all went to a bar in Hale and then to a pub and every one of us was drunk. I remember falling over on the way home from our night out as we were all walking back to Katherine's house as we were all staying the night there. I stayed in the house all day after phoning in sick. I'm now at the point where my drinking and the abuse is affecting my work life. I just stayed in my bedroom and I didn't speak to Anthony apart from when he intermittently came into my bedroom to be abusive. I went into work the next day and carried on trying to work and keep my job. I remember Shirley asking me if I was capable of working and should I not be on the sick before you do something wrong. I don't know what she meant by that but she was the one who reported me. She actually reported me for drinking at work which I didn't do and this was not proved in the three day court case against me. Stuart Cox was also involved in this. I was told to go out to my car, by the management at the NHS, if I at all felt upset as the toilets were very small and we were in an open office so others may have heard me. So one piece of information really upset me and that was the fact that Katherine had mentioned at lunch the day before that she had bought herself a filing cabinet. That particular lunch was at a pub in the Ski Centre and it was late in the afternoon. She met up with me and her friend Jane Heathfield. I had got chatting to Katherine and this is when she mentioned the filing cabinet. I immediately felt sick, like I had been stabbed through the heart. This impacted on me heavily as she was the most disorganised person who I had ever known and yes you may say that she really needed one but she wouldn't have ever bought one for herself. She wasn't that kind of person it would have never entered her head that she was so untidy and she had been in her home for over six years. All her money went on dresses from Vanilla an expensive dress shop in Hale. The reason this upset me was because I already had the suspicions about her and Anthony and the first present he had ever bought me, wait for it, was a filing cabinet as previously mentioned. I thought at the time it was a strange present for him to buy me but I always believed that Anthony had OCD and it was a present to organise me. Part of his control tactics. It may have been a coincidence but I don't believe in them. This incident was later brought into the investigation where she signed it as a true statement saying that when she arrived at the Ski Centre Bar she was late and had driven there. She said she was late because her car hadn't started and that the others, myself and Jane Heathfield, had eaten lunch. The first words in the statement were that Tyff was drunk and drinking more and that Katherine decided to leave. She goes on to say that a bar person came over with three halves of lager of which Tyff drank all three. Katherine then said she sat and watched me drink all three glasses of lager i.e. one and a half pints. She further went on to say in her statement that I then started to talk to two strange men and she said they looked uncomfortable so then she said that she spoke to them and told them that Tyff is drunk. In her next paragraph she states that "Tyff told us that she was going to see a man next week and we said to Tyff that we were worried about her seeing this man on her own". So it was ok for her to leave me drunk with two men I had never met, knowing I was driving from the Ski Centre Bar to my mum's house in Marple Bridge which is at least a thirty minute drive away. I have to ask myself why my friend let me, as she described, drive home and drive a vehicle without trying to stop me or report me to the police. She gave an image of me being out of control on drink. She hadn't even tried to offer help. This isn't my recollection of events.

My story is that I had lunch and one glass of wine and then drove home to my mum's safely. I remember saying hello to two men but don't remember saying any more. She has depicted me as being in a drunken stupor and chatting up two men then driving drunk up the motorway for about thirty to forty minutes. She then said in her statement that she had telephoned me later to check I had got home ok and she said that I was at home and was fine. This is confusing and is also a lie. I did not drink that amount and I left the Ski Centre totally fine and able to drive the journey home. In a different part of her statement to the internal investigation team she said that Tyff had drunk and driven home but only on a couple of occasions and didn't drink a lot. You are probably as confused as I am by her behaviour. She contradicts herself in her statement many times but this was never raised in the internal investigation. She also said that my drink driving had got out of control which totally contradicts her other statement. I was amazed that no one within the NHS internal investigation raised these issues. They just let it go.

The other thing that was interesting (in her statement) was that Jane Heathfield and Katherine were very concerned about me seeing this fictitious man. They were quite happy to leave me drunk, in the possession of a car, with two men. Yet they were very worried about me seeing this man in the future that didn't exist. I was totally confused myself by now. Katherine should have known if not on a personal level but as her capacity as a professional physiotherapist that she has to identify and minimise risk. You must not do anything, or allow someone else to do anything, which could put the health and safety of a service user, carer or colleague at unacceptable risk. So she sat and watched me, so she says in her evidence in her statement, get drunk, drink even more and then leave me drunk in a bar with two strange men, knowing that I would be driving home. This, as a friend, alone is despicable behaviour and also a Professional Body registrant has to manage risk and you must take reasonable steps to reduce the risk of harm to service users and colleagues as far as possible. So in this situation her evidence makes her out to be totally irresponsible and uncaring about her colleague and friend. If this evidence was true I would have said that I have to take blame here too but this was a total fabrication of the event. If that had been me and she was as her evidence stated I would certainly have taken her car keys, given her some coffee, told the bar staff not to serve her and would have driven her home safely. I felt at the time that she would have been quite happy for me to have driven home and hurt someone or killed myself. All the issues were going through my head and the more I thought about all of the things she had done to me the worse I became.

That night I got home to my mum's house after having lunch with them both I was devastated and I did drink about two to three glasses of wine as it was all going around in my head that my so called best friend had been seeing my husband behind my back for God knows how long. How I felt is just beyond words. How could she do this to me after all the help I had given her over the years of our friendship? Whenever she felt upset she would come to my home and we would sit and talk for hours with me trying to help her. I got up the following morning and surprise surprise I felt really sick and could see snow outside. The snow had been falling most of the night and it was not ideal driving conditions and I had to be at work that day. I spoke with my mum telling her that I was devastated and the realisation had set in about Katherine and Anthony. Everything added up all at once all the situations that I had wondered how he had known everything that he had. Mum said that we have to keep going no matter what, so I telephoned work to my support worker to advise I was coming in but the snow was really bad and the traffic was horrendous. I therefore arrived to work late and I had advised my support worker to start handover. I then arrived late to the handover meeting. I felt very numb and could not stomach any breakfast and I must have smelt of alcohol. I completed the handover and then went to my car as I had put some food in there for me. I couldn't face the food so just sat in the car for a while trying to work it all out. I mean it's quite simple now when I look at it but at the time the thought of my best friend for twenty years shagging my husband was heart wrenching. After a while I went back into work to commence the discharge letters for the patients. I remember I hadn't had a wash so I sprayed some perfume on me and went back in to complete the work. I then had a chat with my support worker to say that we had to visit some patients in the afternoon. I remember going out to the car again as I was trying to control my emotions and could feel myself welling up and I had been told that this was what I should do by the management. I felt sick, couldn't eat and sat there for quite a while. Even though Anthony had been a total bastard with his beatings and abuse, I quite astonishingly still loved the man. It's like an addiction in a way; you love someone you shouldn't be loving as they are so horrible to you. Once again I came back into the office and tried to work thinking to myself just get through the day and then I can work out what I was going to do next. I remember doing some of the statistics and input this data onto the computer. It was around lunchtime and the next minute my direct line manager and a woman from H.R. Dept. came and took me into a room in private and said that there had been allegations made against me that I had been drinking in the workplace. I was dumbstruck and shocked and remember saying that this is not true. I told them I had been drinking the night before and gave them the reasons why. I said that I felt I was able to work but was told that I could not drive home and my retort was how was I going to get home to my mum's? After a lot of to-ing and fro-ing they allowed my support worker to take me home to Marple Bridge. He came into my mum's home for a cup of tea and then he took a taxi back to work. I had allowed him in for a cup of tea being polite and I later found out that it was he who had reported me. He said that he had smelt alcohol on me and that I had been going out to the car and also said that I wasn't upset. They must have thought that I was going out to the car to drink. There was a full unopened bottle of wine in my car and a bottle of tonic water and I had put this there as my mum did not like any alcohol in her home. I hadn't drunk any alcohol at work. They did not breathalyse me they just took the word of my support worker and Katherine's friend Shirley Ascot. I wondered how he had smelt alcohol on my breath as he hadn't been sitting anywhere near me he had been sitting on the other side of the room. At no point had he ever come near enough to me to smell my breath prior to reporting me. The closest he got to me was in the room to the handover and he was still across the room from me. The last thing I was told was that the NHS would contact me in due course. I wasn't suspended at this time it was a few days later after I sent text messages. I have to laugh as I looked like a total nutcase. I think I was on the edge of the precipice and I was being pushed and pushed and was letting them do it. I was in a complete state of confusion and a complete haze I really don't know how I ended up like this. I just went to bed and kept analysing things over and over in my head. I didn't realise myself at the time that I was on the verge of a nervous breakdown nor did the NHS show any interest as to my wellbeing. Even if I was an alcoholic surely they should have provided some help not condemn me. During the three days before I sent the text messages Katherine stated that she text me and spoke to me regularly and that had arranged to meet on the Thursday for lunch. She then stated that she knew I wasn't eating and drinking in bed and that they wanted me to come over to meet them to go for lunch. (This is actually in her witness statement word for word.) Which of course I didn't do as I had realised it was Katherine having an affair.

She hadn't actually phoned or text me regularly at all and she got rid of all her text messages to me because she said her daughter was coming home to stay with her for a while and she was worried that her daughter in her late twenties may read what we had both sent each other and would be upset. That's her excuse and knowing there would be an investigation she deleted all the texts from her to me but not mine to her. She kept those to show the investigation team. I thought this was quite suspicious that she had deleted all her texts to me but kept mine. She was making out in one statement that I was joining them for lunch as she thought it would be uplifting for me even though she states on the other hand that I was in bed drunk and not eating. I found it strange that if she was so concerned about me why invite me from Marple Bridge to Urmston, a forty minute drive, when I am drinking. Why did she not come to visit me and just go for a coffee at my mum's or a local café?

The following week she had put her statement in about the text messages and she felt very scared and intimidated by me and stated in her statement that she lived alone and her partner at the time was away on a skiing holiday. Strange she didn't go with him as skiing was her all-time favourite hobby. Her partner pays for all her holidays as well he always paid for everything. I knew she was not going out with Matt Harding at the time as she had told me herself. If she had been with him there is no way that she would have missed that skiing holiday as he always paid for it. It was also interesting that she was ringing the house telling my brother she did not have a boyfriend and that she was a single mother and she didn't even like Anthony so why should she be going out with him. My brother came to speak to me saying that I needed to stop this with Katherine as she was on her own and a single mum (by the way her daughter was in her late twenties at the time, had a boyfriend and was buying a house with him).

For some reason my brother was made to think that she had a small child and not an adult one who needed hardly any support. She was trying to get sympathy from my brother and turn him against me by getting him to think that I was lying. I told my brother that her daughter was twenty six and not a small child as he had been led to believe and that her boyfriend was on a skiing holiday. Yet another lie from her I really believe that she manipulated everyone around her at work against me and was a two faced liar who stabbed me in the back. So much of her evidence has been refuted with contradicting evidence from other reputable sources who have said it wasn't true. I can produce evidence to support my truth, however, Katherine had no evidence to back up her lies apart from the texts I sent.

I do admit that these were nasty of me but I was so very angry with her and what she had done. I have never done anything like that before and I did it because I had found out what she and Anthony were up to behind my back. I do still believe that they would have been quite happy if I had of died as they would have got everything. However, Anthony went off with another woman from the Health Club also called Katherine. So she didn't get her man after all sweet justice.

I received a call from the NHS to advise that I was to attend a meeting with Felicity O'Shearon who was the head of Immediate Care and a lady from Human Resources. This was around a week after the text messages. I attended the meeting I sat on my own opposite Felicity with the H.R. Manager stood by the door. I was told that they were considering my actions of texting Katherine and drinking at work as gross professional misconduct. I stated to them that I was the victim and not the perpetrator and thought that I was innocent until I was proved guilty. They took no notice of me and told me that they would like me to go to Occupational Health and they were making the arrangements and I thought this meant that I was going to get some help.

Felicity advised me that I was being suspended on full pay but I must admit that my feeling was that they had already made their minds up that I was guilty. I admitted to the text messages and the reasons why but no one believed me as Katherine was an extremely good liar, let's face it, she had lied to all of her friends, after having relationships with their husbands and had got away with it or so she thought. I left the meeting feeling one step off the floor and without anyone listening to me or what I had to say in defence of my actions. I did attend the appointments with Occupational Health and all they did was take my blood I feel to get evidence against me for having alcohol in my blood. I had already been honest and told them that I had had some drinks the evening before I came to work. They offered no further help and said it was up to me to instigate that. They knew I was a victim of domestic violence as they had given me the time off for an hours counselling from the domestic violence team. At the time of the counselling I worked at a hospital in Stretford and was deemed fit to be at work on the days of my appointments. I left work to get to my appointment in Old Trafford probably five to ten minutes away. My routine was to drive from work to the appointment, park up, enter the building and sign in, enter the lift up to the third floor and then sit down in the offices and wait for my appointment. Bear in mind that Katherine had stated in her true witness statements that I had gone there and arrived drunk. I then had a full hour of counselling. As stated earlier I have the evidence from the Domestic Violence Charity to say that I wasn't at any time drunk. I was treated like a leper and a liar without any evidence apart from the texts which I admitted to.

The outcome of this meeting was that I was going to be fully investigated as at that time the allegations were drinking at work and sending abusive texts to a colleague and a phone call to a family member. They had me banged to rights on the texts and phone call as I openly admitted that I would win in the end and if she wanted the dirty bastard she was welcome to him and also that I was going to destroy her as she had tried to destroy me. I believe she was scared of me finally finding out the truth about her that witness statements now had to be taken from the various colleagues involved in the work place. However, before any of the witness statements had been taken I was informed by my Manager in the meeting that this was gross professional misconduct and that I was guilty. I told them that I was a victim and that I had never drank at work but had drank often on the evenings before. I have to hold my hands up that I had a drink problem and why I had sunk this low. I advised that I was never off sick and always paid attention to my work.

The NHS commenced their own investigation and were busy taking witness statements and gaining evidence against me. Interestingly, one of the witness statements from my Support Worker mentioned that I had stated weeks before the 20th January that I thought that it was Katherine having an affair with my husband. He replied that Katherine had told him she didn't like Anthony so how could it be her. He also stated that he knew I had been reading the Liberty book and that I had made Anthony fit the description of an abusive man from the book. I was actually reading the book to help me understand Anthony's abusive behaviours.

I had already made up my mind that it was Katherine having the affair because of the punching incident in my hallway when she stood and watched him punch me in the face with glasses on and did nothing. Also the situation about the filing cabinet, just a minute while I have a laugh. I knew that the majority of her statement was lies and was unable to prove it at the time. She also made out that it was me that was doing all the lying about Anthony's abuse towards me. Also there were numerous other times that she claimed I was drunk. Evidence that I have since obtained has proved that she is a liar. There were so many holes in her evidence that the NHS never investigated and just automatically believed her and it is my opinion that they wanted rid of me because of my drink problem. Instead of offering me help they just started to dig a hole for my grave to put me in. I did not feel supported in any way by my manager and considering that I had worked for the NHS for a total of thirty two years had expected some form of help. The only colleague who tried to support me was my Union Representative who tried very hard indeed to help. They never offered any information on any services that could help me with my drink problem or the marriage abuse. I went on my own to my GP and asked for a referral to Alcohol and drug team. I started to attend the counselling for the domestic violence, I had previously been to these but couldn't make the appointments because I had to work. I did make the effort to go to as many as possible even going on the bus due to my right arm being in plaster.

Because I was still living in the abusive situation within the marriage my drinking improved habits were like being on a roller coaster. A little at times but then large amounts at others. I could never get my freedom from the drink within the marriage. Even when I tried not to drink he would be at me all the time about my drinking. He never let up about it and often drank to excess in front of me.

Prior to the suspension, I was living at my mum's, none of my so called friends came to visit and I was treated like a leper. Alcoholics often get this treatment from those around them as people don't understand it. It is a recognised illness but ordinary people don't recognise that or what a person may have had to go through to end up an alcoholic. People look down on you as if you are one of the dregs of society. A little story about addiction: many years ago an experiment took place using a rat in a large cage with heroin and water. Basically the rat dies, poor thing, every time as it keeps going for the heroin. Recent experiments using rats again, which were put in a large cage with balls and toys with wheels and some other rats for companionship, connection and fun. The rats were also given water and heroin again they weren't fed this it was just put there. What do you think happened? They all lived happily ever after. None of them died and none of them went for the heroin. In my case I found a new playground I left the marriage gained new friends, hobbies, creative activities, career change and I have not drank for two and a half years. There haven't been any instances where I have wanted to drink even though I have gone through extremely stressful times with the court cases etc. I understand addictive desire now and it is quite interesting as it is called AD and I gave it the name Arthur Daley, a conman, so when I get thoughts I know the thoughts will go and I don't act on them. The addiction manifests from the amagdela based within the brain, where the addictive desire is held and is about the size of a kidney bean. The amagdela can't walk to the shops to buy alcohol but tries to tell you that if you have another drink it will be ok so basically it is trying to con you into going to the shops to buy more drink. You can prevent this working by changing the thought and not acting on it. You have to be so strong and learn that you are powerless over alcohol.

When you are drinking you isolate yourself from everyone else and in my humble opinion part of the way to sobriety is to remove all negative influences and energy sucking vampires from my life. I removed them and replaced with loving, caring, compassionate friends who supported me and loved me better and these were June Axon, Susan Bean and Lynn Gaskell. They never gave up on me often visiting my mum's house with little gifts, one was a little owl with a solar light to watch over me at night. What a difference from the absolute horror of Katherine who was always encouraging me to go to pubs etc. Even buying me drinks, large ones at that, which I often thought was on purpose. She knew if I had a drink that Anthony would kick off and I would be in trouble and the violence would follow. How could she do this to her friend of over twenty years? I will tell you why she wanted my husband, our large house, and all the trimmings. Even at work she showed jealousy and she would avoid work if she could and her colleagues knew this as I did. I actually did her work for her when she was getting divorced from Dennis her ex-husband. I would go in and do the work while she stayed in the car as she couldn't cope with the work at the same time as her divorce.

In my witness statement I said that I knew Katherine was having an affair with my husband and I had also stated that she had seen the violence when she set me up and Anthony punched me in the face. I had mentioned about the evidence from the Hotel Manager recording the beating that Anthony gave me in Greece. Katherine definitely knew about this as she went for counselling, about her divorce, with Katy Smith, a lovely woman, but had suffered horrendous abuse by being raped by four men who dragged her off her bike whilst going to work. I also went with Katherine on one occasion and said to Katy that I would like some counselling because my husband had beaten me up in Greece and this was in front of Katherine. I can't get the evidence from Katy Smith to support me on this as she has left the Trust many years ago and she wrote a book about the NHS and about how badly they had looked after her after her rape. They would allow her to come in at later times than her normal hours because she struggled in the mornings with depression, which was hardly surprising after her ordeal. That is the only thing that work ever did to help her. No-one at work actually knew about this as she never told anyone. Just like me as I didn't tell many people either what was going on inside my home. When I did mention it Katherine told everyone that I was lying and that Anthony was bad but not that bad. This was in her witness statement. I couldn't believe what she had said in her statements there were lies throughout it.

During the time of this long lasting investigation which went on for months and months I felt so lonely and depressed. I talked to my mum and brother who gave me so much support. My other brother helped in his way. I spent most of the time crying in bed it was a horrible time for me. I felt it was the end of everything in my life that I had known. I didn't realise at the time that this was the beginning of my road to recovery and a new wonderful life. I had reached the lowest ebb in my life. One particular night I remember I was in the depth of depression and felt perhaps my life was ending. Every thought process I had that night was negative and actually some people do kill themselves at this point in their life. I was extremely lucky and grateful as I survived this awful night which is called the Dark Night of the soul which is explained in a book about assertiveness for light workers. Because I was a people pleaser all my life I was not an assertive person so I swung from being a passive person to being a really aggressive person with my ex-husband. I was either a mouse or a lion neither of which were any good.

The investigation was still ongoing by April 2013 and I was by now completely traumatised as nothing I had said was believed. I was then asked to go in to work for a sickness review. The evening before I was staying at a friend's house and I had got up in the night as I couldn't sleep with the worry. I went downstairs for a coffee and was quite surprised when my friend's husband appeared. He asked if I was alright and I said that I was just making a coffee. He then asked if I would make him one too so I did. We sat in the kitchen and I felt really awkward as he was saying nasty things about his wife to me. She was a wonderful person and a dear friend to me so I wasn't happy about this at all. I noticed a bottle of wine sitting on the floor so I picked it up and had a couple of large glasses. I was completely unable to cope with the situation as my friend had been very good and supportive to me. He knew I had a drink problem and I tried so hard to think straight but it didn't work. To cut a long story short I went to the meeting the next day not feeling I was over the limit. However, work quite rightly, phoned the police and they were waiting for me outside work. I only drove out the side road around the corner from the hospital and the police pulled me up immediately. They breathalysed me and of course I was over the limit and was prosecuted. I received an eighteen month ban reduced to twelve months as I attended a course. You can imagine I felt even worse as I was living at my mum's house, buying a house in Flixton, without having the use of my car. The whole thing was a real mess. It taught me a big lesson as I had to catch the bus for a year and it shocked me into the realisation that I just could not drink. This helped cement the fact that the drink was ruining my life and was having a bad effect on those around me but at this time I was so ill I couldn't think of anything apart from just trying to get through the day.

I moved into my new home in May 2013 and then I had to attend yet another final day of investigating. All the people who were involved were stood huddled together in a little group. I was surprised at Katherine as she cried all the way through so I couldn't ask her any questions in my defence. Good tactic on her part. At the end of the meeting and the day, I thought they were going to make a decision, however, I thought wrongly as to my surprise they were all going on holiday and they advised it would not re-convene for another five weeks. They also brought additional evidence in and that was to do with phone calls. However, my Union Representative telephoned the Chartered Society of Physiotherapists, in London and they were unhappy with the fact that this evidence had been brought in late, i.e. seven months later, and it was something to do with phone calls. This had now been going on for seven months without any decisions being made and I now had to wait yet another five weeks. I was so desperate, tired, depressed and alone and so very, very sad that my best friend and my husband could have planned my destruction. I just gave up and said that I would retire. It was accepted that day and it went no further. I only did this because I was tired of fighting with no support other than the Union Representative. My friend Jill came with me that day and sat downstairs waiting for me. Funnily enough she could see a lot of people going about their business and someone put a load of paperwork in the bin whilst she was sat watching them and she nosily picked it out of the bin to have a look and it was confidential information about me and phone calls.

Throughout this whole process my manager had referred my case to the Professional Body based in London. They are the Professional Body governing over fitness to practice. I started to receive mail from them whilst going through the internal investigation and my divorce. To be quite honest I couldn't cope with it all at the time so I decided to concentrate on my divorce for a while to obtain my half of the funds for the house. After a long drawn out battle with Anthony trying to blacken my name and have all the domestic violence information removed from the divorce petition I was left completely drained. It had taken every bit of energy I had to fight to have this remain and eventually I had it put back into the petition. That was the reason I was divorcing him it wasn't about all the adultery.

The next step after the house purchase was to sort my pension out as I had retired now. I had a lot to sort out before I could even think about the Professional Body. I had to sell my car which I then used to pay rent to my brother as he bought my house for me until I had the divorce settlement in place. It was so difficult to prove who I was because Anthony wouldn't let me have my birth certificate although he had previously let me have my passport which was in the bags he delivered. I finally sorted out my pension, sold the car, paid my brother a year's rent until I could get the house sold. I moved into my new home in May 2013; a new step to freedom. I was starting my new life in my new home and I was so excited about moving in. I started to decorate, stamping my own personality on it and was helped by my friend Jill.

I began going dancing with my friends June and Sue. I had stopped drinking by now with the help of my friends and the associations I became involved with. My life was gradually being rebuilt into my new life. The healing process had begun even though there were still some enormous hurdles for me to jump.

The divorce was still ongoing whilst moving into my new home and Anthony was putting every obstacle possible in my way to prevent me from getting a divorce. It wasn't that he wanted to stay with me he just didn't want to lose the house. He would not allow me to have any photographs of my children at all, any jewellery, or any personal items out of the house. Hence the egg episode mentioned earlier which I still find hilarious, I threw eggs at my own house, damaged my own garden, and no one was even in the house. Yet he could beat the living daylights out of me for years and I couldn't get anyone to help or believe me. I spoke to the police and they went to my home and requested my gold jewellery. Anthony told the police that I didn't own any except some old box which he went and got. It was one of my old old jewellery boxes with bits of rubbish in it basically. The police brought it to me and said there was nothing else they could do. In the end as a last resort I had my solicitor send him letters requesting the items must be returned. He knew this would cost me more money. Just more hassle for me and more money for the solicitors. Anthony then wrote to the Professional Body to request that I be struck off the register and look at my fitness to practice. This was done on the 30 October 2013, just after the egg episode. Interestingly, in the financial statements, I eventually received, he was in the Swan, a public house, in Altrincham, Cheshire on the 25th October 2013 and spent twenty nine pounds fifty. I would say a meal for two and what a coincidence that Katherine just lives minutes away from that pub. It is an out of the way pub in a place known as Little Bollington. In all the years I lived with him we knew no one in Altrincham, apart from Katherine. The other girlfriend he was seeing also called Katherine lived in Swinton. As Anthony and Katherine had stated that they weren't having an affair and he said he was actually seeing the squash player Katherine, with the same name, in Swinton so why would he go all the way out to Altrincham to have something to eat as there are some lovely places in Worsley and Swinton areas. Just all too much of a coincidence for me and I don't believe in them. From the financial statements, he used to frequent places in Monton, Worsley which is where Katherine, squash player, lived.

Then suddenly three days later Anthony sends a letter to the Professional Body with information about me which he could only have obtained from Katherine. The other girl in Swinton didn't know anything about me. Only Katherine could have furnished him with the details. It didn't get him anywhere because the Professional Body said there was no case to answer. I thought it interesting that if he had managed to have me struck off at that stage in the proceedings then it wouldn't have been taken any further and Katherine would then not have been subjected to giving evidence against me. In his letter he clearly stated my case reference number for the Professional Body case. There was no way in which he would have had access to that information. Also he knew all about the case and that I had stated that my marriage was marred with violence and controlling behaviour which was in the case papers which were confidential. He could have only have found that out from Katherine. He may also have opened any mail that had been sent there by the Professional Body for me by mistake. It would have had private and confidential on it. He had actually forwarded on my mail and none of it had been opened. Therefore, in my summation, it must have come from Katherine as there was no other possible way. My work place knew that I wasn't living at my marital address anymore but apparently it was my responsibility to let the Professional Body know. He also claimed in his letter that I had gone to a friend's house and asked for a lift into work because I was drunk. This was not true and what had actually happened was I had gone on a Monday morning in my car to my colleague's house Shirley Ascott and I told her when I got there that I was traumatised and I had been drinking over the weekend as my husband had been abusive towards me. I was confused and didn't really know if I should be going to work. Shirley Ascot rang my support worker to get advice and he advised that I should go home and ring in sick. Interestingly my husband would have been at work so how does he know about this? Shirley and Katherine were also really good friends outside work so I believe that she told Katherine and Katherine told Anthony to get me into trouble. He also put in the letter that I had endangered his life and that of my son and step-daughter by drinking whilst driving. This wasn't true and anyone would ask the same question as I did, in that, why didn't he drive and why did he let my son and his daughter get in the car if I was drunk as he has written. This made me laugh as the other witnesses also said the same things. That they had got in cars with me driving when I was drunk. Why would you do that? Because of course they were lying. I never took any of them anywhere in my car. He went on to mention many more issues about me in work and about my work colleagues but he didn't know any of my work colleagues apart from Katherine.

The final outcome of it all was that I was granted a divorce on his unreasonable behaviour. I had mixed feelings about this. I was devastated on the one hand but also truly relieved on the other as I didn't have to suffer any more abuse. However, I truly loved Anthony for many years and I regretted losing my son who was under Anthony's spell and control now.

Whilst the divorce was going on I volunteered at a local charity shop for twelve months thinking that I wanted to get back to the good person that I was before the alcohol. I also did other volunteer work taking other addicts swimming and doing some voluntary counselling about my experiences. I felt I wanted to give back to society something that I had taken by my alcohol abuse.

I was training at this point in time as a complimentary therapist and was also setting up my own business; providing complimentary therapies from home and also going mobile to client's homes. Whilst I was doing my training I went along to the Job Centre to see if I could find a job there or if there was any financial help that I may be entitled to. However, I was advised that I wasn't entitled to any benefit. I said that I really wanted to know about the Business Enterprise Allowance as I was starting my own business. I wrote a business plan in Manchester with an adviser and they were a great help and I completed my business plan and some business cards. I was awarded the New Business Enterprise Allowance which was for the first six months. This really helped me and I bought some of my equipment with the money such as my therapy bed and some portable hot stones and some oils. This was expensive stuff; the stones alone were four hundred pounds. I managed really well and had the majority of what I needed to start my practices. I started off really well but it was hard at the same time. It wasn't bringing in enough money for me to live so I applied for a job doing the same thing. I work with Angels, this is my choice, I don't expect anyone else to understand, but I follow their signs which are given to me in the form of numbers. For instance I was driving to my friend Laney's house and I would see 444. This means that the Angels are around me at that time and they were letting me know that Laney was truly my friend. Whilst I was sitting with Laney in her dining room and we were writing this book I saw a 777 on the end of a phone number. The meaning of 777 is that I have listened to divine guidance and I am where I am supposed to be and that I will receive miracles in my life. I have also seen 999 twice which means that we are doing light workers work and also endings and conclusions. I see lots of different numbers which have various meanings but they guide me through. These numbers usually repeat themselves several times to reinforce the meaning. I started to write the numbers down and would go onto the numerology websites to find their meanings. It may sound wacky to you but it works for me perfectly and many others that I know. Throughout this time I was working out who I was and that I had started leaning towards healing work. I am actually called an empath which is normally an old soul. You will find empaths working with people, animals or nature with a true passion and dedication to help them. They are often tireless teachers and/or caretakers for our environment and all within it. Many volunteers are empathic and give up personal time to help others without pay and/or recognition. There is a great deal more to describe an empath which can be looked up on the internet.

When I was providing a counselling service to others, each with their own individual problems, we would often all go on organised walks. When on the walks I would regularly talk to people about how I had maintained my sobriety and the help I had received. Along the walks I always saw white feathers. You may say that they could have come from birds but there weren't any birds when I looked around. This is a common sign that the Angels are around us and supporting us. You only have to ask and then when you receive help be kind and considerate and say thank you. This happened on many many occasions and I always found a five pence piece or a penny in the changing rooms or on the way when I was taking people swimming. I provided help to people on a voluntary basis. I felt this was an affirmation from the Angels to show me that I was on the right path. Wherever I went I always found money. I often saw the number 555 at this time and the meaning behind this number indicates that there is big changes which are coming and to prepare for them.

# CHAPTER 7

## Fitness to practice hearings

In October 2013 Anthony had tried very hard to get me struck off as a practicing physiotherapist. After egg gate Anthony was somewhat annoyed with me but when wasn't he? He was always annoyed at everything I did. I bet steam was venting out of his ears. He had put this into the complaint and also said in his letter that I was driving around drunk and going to colleague's homes asking for lifts. This wasn't actually true. The only person that knew I had visited a colleague's home, as I was so traumatised and not drunk, would have been Shirley Ascott who was Katherine's work colleague and friend. It may have been Stuart Cox, my support worker, as Shirley had made a phone call to him whilst I was at her home. My solicitor wrote a letter explaining why I had thrown the eggs and that it was a personal and one off event. The Professional Body looked at Anthony's complaint and carried out an investigation and my solicitor had to write a letter of support for me. The ending was that the Professional Body said there was no case to answer. However, I did have the criminal record for egg gate. It would have been 40-Love at this point.

He had used an incident where I had been trying to escape from another beating and had tried to climb out of my bedroom window. Unfortunately, I fell and broke my wrist. I had actually been drinking and will hold my hand up to that. Anthony said it was my fault and I had fallen out of the window due to drinking which isn't true. Everyone else thought I had tried to kill myself which I hadn't. This incident actually made me realise that I needed help so I went to an alcohol and drug team for alcohol abuse and dependency counselling but I could only attend on a Friday morning due to work. I had to go on the bus as I had no licence and also had my arm in plaster so I could only attend for a short time. I did, however, receive a certificate to say that I had attended and sought help. Anthony sent these certificates to the Professional Body to reinforce that I was just an alcoholic and shouldn't be practicing. However, this actually went against him and it backfired as they saw this as me trying to get help and support so the case was thrown out with no case to answer at that point. I was now playing at advantage to Anthony and if I won the next point I win the game. In one of my text messages to Katherine I stated that I would win in the end. I believe in the truth, there are only three things that we can't hide from in this life, one is the moon, and one is the sun and finally the truth.

I was already facing a tribunal in London later that year brought about by the NHS against me. My feelings are that Anthony had taken this action against me to protect Katherine so she would not have to testify in the hearing. The Professional Body as mentioned previously is not a criminal court but a Professional Body that looks at individual's fitness to practice. Such as dishonesty, confidentiality or lack of, managing risk, personal conduct, integrity and a long list of others. The allegations were drinking at work, sending abusive texts to my colleague Katherine, in January in the course of one week and the drink driving was four months later.

Katherine had asked for her witness statement to be held on Skype so she would be in Manchester giving her evidence and I would be in the court room in London. She had said she wished to do this because she was frightened of me, which I had thought very strange as she had stopped at the bus stop and talked to me to find out how I was and she even asked me if I had a boyfriend. So how could she be so scared of me now? In my opinion she had only stopped at the bus stop to find out what I was doing to advise Anthony.

I defended myself via my solicitor by way of letter to the Professional Body to put forward my explanation as I did not understand why she was so scared of me. I then had to go to London which was basically there and back in a day. I had to put forward my evidence to the panel and Katherine was allowed to give evidence by Skype. The other witness, Stuart Cox, was also allowed to give evidence on Skype as he said he had a bad knee and was awaiting an operation and worried that it might be on the day I was in court. The investigating officer is the only person apart from me that attended the hearing and in her investigation had stated that I had drunk at work even though she had no evidence and that there was no evidence that Katherine was having an affair with my husband. The only investigating she did was to obtain statements from Katherine's two friends who were my work colleagues. She did not check up on any of the evidence provided to ensure it was the truth. Katherine had said that I was going to my domestic violence appointments drunk. She had not made a phone call or written to ask the domestic violence team if this was a true statement. I now have the evidence myself to prove that this was a complete lie made up by Katherine to make me look worse than I was. I have a written letter from Woman's Charity which is the women's organisation where I went for help and this states that on no occasion did I ever turn up inebriated to appointments or sound inebriated on the phone. I did a twelve week course plus three months counselling there so it was about six months in total and a lot of appointments and many phone calls.

I had sent the abusive text in January 2013, the final three day hearing was not until 2014. In between these times I was standing at the bus stop waiting for the bus, it was a Wednesday morning, and I was on the way to Manchester for a course that I was taking with the alcohol and drug team to help me move into a normal life. When Katherine drove past, she surprisingly pulled up, got out of her car and began a conversation with me. She was in her uniform so was obviously working. I was quite shocked at this because of all the previous animosity towards me from her and she asked me such a stupid question I nearly burst out laughing. She had told everyone that she was frightened of me. She said nothing more to me other than had I found myself a new boyfriend which I thought was really strange. I then asked about Anne her twin sister and that I was missing her as we had

had such a long friendship and I also asked about Jane Heath-field. She replied that they were both fine and that she was talk-ing to her twin again after nearly a year. (After Katherine had an affair with her twin's husband.) She then got back in her car and carried on with her journey. She wasn't scared of me then and I never saw her again until the hearing when she said she was scared to be in the same room as me. If this was true then why had she stopped at the bus stop? It would have been a per-fect opportunity to have done something to her as we were all alone and no witnesses?

The next event with the Professional Body was in April 2014 for a three day court hearing. I stayed at my friend's house who had moved from Marple Bridge to London. She had a flat and offered me overnight accommodation. She also very kindly drove me to the hearing every day and I was enormously grateful to her for the help she gave me.


*Day 1 – Professional Body Hearing*

I was in a room with about ten other persons, two solicitors one of which was representing the Professional Body and a further one brought in by the Professional Body to ensure that due pro-cess is carried out, three members of the lay panel, one of which was a doctor and one a physiotherapist not sure what the other one was but she was sat in the middle of the other two, meet and greet lady, the stenographer and myself and then the witnesses. I was advised to take a barrister with me but I had no option but to represent myself, how could I afford that, or even a solicitor? I thought to myself I know what went on so I can represent my-self. This first day was the most stressful of all. I could hardly eat I just lived off coffee.

They advised me what they would be dealing with that day which was the first allegation, namely, the drinking at work al-legation made by Shirley Ascott, Occupational Therapist, Stuart Cox, and support worker.

The investigating officer had come to the hearing from Manchester and basically gave her evidence which was extremely flawed. As I didn't know what was to be said about me I hadn't prepared well enough and didn't have some of the crucial evidence I needed in support of myself. She gave her evidence based on the two colleagues, friends of Katherine's -without any investigation. They hadn't breathalysed me, no blood tests had been carried out at that time, only that they thought I had been drinking as I had gone out to my car several times and they could smell alcohol on my breath but this was from the night before.

My defence to her allegations was that I had been going out to my car as I was so traumatised at the time and I had been advised by the management that I was allowed to do this as they knew I was going through a traumatic divorce case and that I had regular outbursts of tears. We worked in an open plan office and the toilets were very public so if I was sat in there crying everybody would know. I also said that I had been drinking the night before as I had realised that I was right about Katherine and my husband and was devastated.

Stuart Cox, the support worker, gave evidence on Skype. When I was allowed to question him I said to him that I was a victim of domestic violence as he well knew and he just went Huh. He had a smirk on his face as if I was making it all up. So I wondered at that moment what Katherine or Shirley Ascott had been telling him. Whilst I was on Skype with him I said to Stuart that I had mentioned the fact that I suspected Katherine of having an affair with my husband when we were out together working in his vehicle. He stated that he didn't think it was possible as she had told him that she didn't like Anthony. He then went on to say that he did not think it was professional of me to have mentioned that to him in the car (although he had been talking about me to everyone else). The panel then began questioning Stuart Cox about the morning when the allegations were made. They asked where he was sat in relation to me in the office. Were you sat face to face with Tyffany or at a distance? He had to admit that he was sat at the other side of the office to me and even in our hand over he was still sat at the other end of the office which is a distance away. They then said to him how could he have smelt alcohol on me when he was nowhere near me? The panel went through all the evidence submitted throughout the day and an HR representative gave evidence on Skype.

Four witnesses had now given their evidence against me apart from Katherine she was due to give her evidence on the next day. I was continually bombarded with the bundle of evidence against me which was about ten inches high. I said to the panel I don't need any of the bundle as I can remember it all very clearly. I thought to myself just because you all think I'm a nutcase I have a very high IQ and a really good memory. I would never forget Anthony punching me in the face while Katherine stood and watched him do it with that horrible expression on her face and that she made no attempt to help me. I will never forget that.

The panel then went out to make their decision about this day's allegation. They were gone for about two hours so I just sat there waiting and feeling dreadful. I was shaking with nerves knowing that the witnesses had lied and their evidence was very flawed and based on what Katherine had been telling them about me and could not be supported with any evidence. Also all the evidence given by the witnesses and myself was done so on oath. My friend Jill was allowed to sit with me and I was so glad she was with me.

I was then brought back into the hearing room and I was shaking with nerves and I went to my chair and saw a white feather on the chair. There were two men and one woman on the panel and the woman spoke addressing me with my full title and stated that this allegation had been looked at in depth by the panel and that there was no evidence in support of these allegations and therefore not proved. I was so relieved but was so nervous I didn't dare show my elation at that point. Little did they know but when I went to the toilet I used my pendulum, which I always carry with me, and it had indicated that I would be found innocent.

When I was out of the vicinity I was so happy and felt like jumping for joy but controlled myself as it wasn't over yet there were two more days to get through. This was now a year and a half later and I hadn't been able to work as a physio as how could I get a job as I needed a reference. At this time I was only fifty four and could have worked until I was of retirement age. I was so looking forward to questioning Katherine about her evidence the next day I couldn't sleep much thinking about it and mulling it over in my mind.

That evening I went back to Jill's flat with her and was on such a high. I hadn't felt this way for such a long time. I was so elated even though I was not practicing at the time as a physiotherapist it was a matter of principle to me as my work was very important to me but I knew I needed help and the NHS never offered me any at all. Jill made a meal for us with her partner and we sat down and discussed the day. They were both really chuffed for me that this hadn't been proved.


*Day 2 – Professional Body Hearing*

Again the Professional Body solicitor read out the next allegation which was the text messages and harassment of Katherine's dad. I told the hearing that I was guilty of sending the text messages and that at the time I was absolutely traumatised as I knew it was her that was having an affair with my husband and that they planned to get me into trouble. The text messages I sent to her were whilst I was on my day off on a Thursday. It was my time and the only mistake I made was using my work phone. I didn't have my own phone as I was living at my mum's and Anthony wouldn't let me take anything out of the house. The NHS accepted the money for private phone calls and I had paid them a bill of thirty pounds previously. This had now been used against me saying I should not have used the work phone. However, I was never advised not to use the work phone and they had accepted the money on the previous occasion.

This was an easier day for me as I admitted to sending the text messages to Katherine. I had sent her quite a lot but I was not rationally thinking at the time with all that had gone on up to this point. The day was more about Katherine giving her evidence on Skype and she gave her testimony saying that I was a liar and everything I had said was lies. I challenged her and asked her why she got out of her car at the bus stop incident if she was so frightened of me. Her reply was that she saw me and it was done on an impulse basis. The truth actually being that if she was as frightened of me as she had said she would have seen me and just drove off. I then questioned her about how her twin sister Anne had found out where I lived as this address was supposed to be protected because of the violence and abuse from Anthony so he could not find out where I am living. However, he had found out through the leaked document from the Child Support Agency that had gone to his solicitor to prove I was paying child support. He had found out by pure accident from his solicitor. I actually believe that he then told Katherine who then told Anne her sister. That is the only possible explanation as nobody else knew where I actually lived. I questioned her further and asked if she had remembered the incident where he had punched me in the face and how he knew I would be home at that specific time. As it was my belief that she had phoned him from her home to let him know she was taking me home. He was at football with our son as he always was and never ever before had come home early. She just sat there on the Skype and would not answer the question. The panel asked her many questions about the phone calls that I had made to gain some perspective on what had been said in the actual phone calls. She said she telephoned my brother John to ask him to stop the phone calls from me. She stated to my brother that she was a single parent and that she had a boyfriend so why would she be interested in Anthony. I highlighted to the panel that this was ridiculous as she was actually a parent to a 26 year old daughter who was buying a house with her boyfriend and would be moving out of her mother's house.

I knew Katherine didn't have a boyfriend at this time as she had told me that they had finished in November and that is why she was not on the skiing holiday with him. In her testimony she stated that her partner had gone skiing without her. My brother was totally taken in by her as many people were as she was a really convincing liar but she often forgot what she had said on previous occasions. She didn't have the memory to be a good liar. He asked me to stop making the phone calls as she is a single parent on her own. I said to my brother John not to make me laugh saying she is older than me and her daughter is in her late twenties. She has her own home, her own car and a really good job so she wasn't the single parent she was painting herself to be and she was just trying to get empathy from him and make me out to be the liar.

After all the evidence had been given on this second day they advised that the judgement would not be made until the following day.

I think that the panel were upset with me as I was asked to apologise to her and I refused. I said she had been sleeping with my husband and trying to ruin my life and lying about me to everyone that she could so there was no way that I was going to apologise. I told them that it perhaps was not the right and wise thing for me to do but I had no regrets with regards to her and I still don't.

Again I went back to Jill's house and just chatted and chilled out as I was quite livid with the audacity that Katherine had shown. I went to bed that evening exhausted after it all and did not sleep. Even Jill said she could hear me moving around the bed tossing and turning. I told her it was because of the alcohol abuse and that no one believed me at work and that Katherine and Anthony stitched me up like a kipper both saying I had made it up. One of their sayings (they both actually said the same saying several times) was that I exaggerate and make it up about Anthony all the time and that I lie all the time. I remember this because Anthony used to come into my mum's house and say "She exaggerates about me all the time it's all lies" and Katherine stated this to me in a phone call to me and she sounded exactly the same as Anthony and it was as though his words were coming out of her mouth.

## Day 3 – Professional Body Hearing

The same procedure followed with the solicitor reading the allegation of drink driving. I accepted that it was my responsibility and I profusely apologised to the panel for my behaviour and I was truly sorry. I told the panel that I was totally traumatised by all the events that were going on in my life and I was also distressed as nobody believed me. I felt like they had got away with it. I explained that since that time I had been on a two day course for drink driving awareness and had learnt from my experience and had to use the bus for one year. So I was aware of the consequences of my actions but I was at the time an alcoholic. The Professional Body's solicitor also said to me that I was parked that day on Trust property. I advised her that she was wrong and that she should relook at her notes as this was incorrect and I was actually parked on the public side road near the Trust Headquarters. I wasn't going out that day to see patients as I was off sick and was going for a work's sickness review to the Trust Headquarters. She went "Oh Oh I will relook at my notes" which she did and then said Tyffany is correct. I then turned to the solicitor and said you need to keep your eye on the ball because I am. I can laugh now at this but I got away with it. At some point during this day she referred back to the first day's allegation to try to reinforce how bad I was. The independent solicitor stopped her dead and said that she could not bring that into this as that has not been proved so you must not refer to this again. She then sat down quietly.

To end the day the panel adjourned for an about three hours and I just sat there waiting and didn't get the final judgement until well after 5pm. I remember sitting with Jill until they finally called me back into the hearing. The female panel member spoke to me and said that with all of the evidence they felt that my fitness to practice had been impaired and that they have to make a sanction. I had retired and wasn't working as a physiotherapist at this time. There are five levels of sanctions that can be given the final one is that you are struck off. The panel gave me the least restriction that they could and they stated that they felt that they believed that I believed that my friend Katherine was having an affair with my husband. They said that there was no evidence for me to substantiate this at this time.

If I had been in possession of Laney's and Dennis's statements at that time it may well have gone very differently for me and Katherine may have been the one answering a fitness to practice hearing.

The final summing up and decision was that I was to be given a six month order where I would have to let an employer know my problems with the alcohol. They accepted the significant in-roads I had made into giving up the alcohol and had been clean for eight months. I had had to provide a significant amount of evidence to prove this. I was advised that I had to write a reflection of my actions and how sorry I am and that I attend support groups and that I need to have some evidence of this, i.e. a signature from a sponsor.

I had gone through all of this trauma to be told I had to do a piece of writing and go to a support group which I was already doing but required the evidence that I had continued with it for about six months. Throughout all of this I could have continued practicing but I hadn't because I was so traumatised by the violence, abuse, deceit, lies, and alcohol.

I stayed overnight at Jill's and we all had a takeaway which I paid for and I had given them money for fuel and some presents for being so kind to me during this awful time. Jill took me for a walk the next day to Windsor. I had a lovely walk round and the day was a bit surreal I remember thinking to myself has all that just really happened? My belief is that the Professional Body had to give me some form of punishment after spending the public purse for three days on this hearing and a day of the previous one and then the one in the next six months.

It was about four months later that I set about writing a letter of reflection where I apologised for my actions and the consequences of drink driving. I did not specify anything about the text messages as to be quite frank I wasn't sorry at all. I couldn't bring myself to apologise for this as it would have been like saying sorry to Katherine and I wasn't and I still hold the same opinion.

The final day, six months later, arrived and I had to travel down to London again. It was yet again very formal with the entire panel there. The solicitor for the Professional Body stood up and advised the hearing that I had sent a letter of reflection but that they had not received a notification that I was going to support groups. I said out loud to her very clearly "but you have got a copy because I have mine here with me". She then looked further into the file and finally found it. Then someone on the panel asked me how I got the letter and who had written it. I then asked if they meant was it in my handwriting. They replied yes. I said that it was because my sponsor could not make the journey today as she has just had major heart surgery and was too ill and eighty five years old so I had written the letter and she had signed it for me. Finally they accepted this. I was then allowed to give my summing up speech. I'm not sure they were aware that I could have got an Oscar for speaking publicly but I had written notes on what I wanted to say. I bet they were all sat their thinking what a crackpot I can't wait to get home today.

I gave a speech on what an empath is in great length and all the traits of an empath. I had used alcohol as a prevention to stop the hurt and pain that I was continuously experiencing with my marriage. I also spoke to the solicitor acting for the professional body saying that I thought she was quite young and very judgmental. I added that my opinion was that until she has been through a prolonged period of domestic violence and abuse for over twenty years she had no right to judge me. Until she had read all information about the subject that she would be a person of limited knowledge and I said that I didn't think she was compassionate or showed empathy. I stated that I now knew who I was and that I really didn't care if they believed me or not but I

161

would still state that Katherine and Anthony conspired against me to make me very ill, to steal my home behind my back, and that they had hoped that I would have drank myself to death as that would have been a very convenient end for me. At the end of this hearing they advised that they had accepted everything I had to say and that I was now fit to practice without any restrictions whatsoever.

What a relief I returned home and carried on with my career with alternative therapies and healing and am so happy doing this. The people within this environment are loving, empathetic, compassionate and help me whilst understanding what I have been through.

I am now free to move on positively with my new life and I have never been so happy. I have new friendships, rekindled old ones and everything is good in my world apart from not having my son with me but I live in hope that one day he will see the truth.

# CHAPTER 8

# My New life

I love my new life and it is full of love and great relationships. There are no arguments or negativities around me anymore great things are happening now. I am experiencing a peaceful, calm and rewarding lifestyle. My home is decorated in all my favourite colours that I love, it is bright and cheery. I work out of an exclusive health club and hotel in Cheshire and I actually love working there. The girls who work at the club are such a lovely bunch and I am very lucky to have such people around me and work in such a great environment. I appreciate everything about it. There are lots of hugs and appreciation from them to me and this is so rewarding. I moved mountains to get here but have proved to myself and others that it can be done.

I have created a healing room within my home where I provide therapies and treatments for private clients and this earns me a small income for which I am truly grateful. I am living my dreams and I have been to Thailand this year with Spice (an activity group based throughout the UK) on a spiritual journey and visited lots of Temples and seen the Gold Buddha. I also do work for Spice working in their Pamper Afternoons about twice a year with my colleague June. There are many Mind, Body and Spirit Fairs that I attend and have the confidence now which I lacked during the years of my marriage. I had it before so I don't know where it went but its back with renewed vigour and energy. These can also be profitable for me and people love my treatments such as Reflexology, Massage, Reiki and Spiritual Healing as this is who I am now.

It was a night of a large super moon I had a stomach ache. Ladies you will understand when I say it was like a period pain but I had not had one of those for at least eighteen months. I took myself off to bed and in the morning I had a large bleed which having some medical knowledge I felt was not right. I looked it up on google, post-menopausal bleeding, and it confirmed my fears that this could be cancer. I took myself off to the doctor that very same day and was examined immediately. The GP agreed with me that I needed to be investigated further. An appointment was made and I attended an appointment at the St. Mary's Hospital in Manchester within two weeks. Initially they did an internal ultra sound scan and acted upon the results by advising that they wanted a biopsy as they found that the endometrial lining had thickened. I went back for a biopsy at St. Mary's and when it was time for my appointment the machine broke. The Consultant asked if he could do an internal sweep of my womb which wasn't as good but at least he would know if there were any abnormal cells. I then waited for the results. I asked the Consultant if positive affirmations would help as I had read a lot on the subject. He advised that it wouldn't do any harm. During this tense time of waiting I started to do daily work with positive affirmations using my healing. I shouted out to the universe each and every day that I was completely well and healthy and there was nothing wrong with me. I did this all the time but specifically performed these at 11.11 which in numerology means new beginnings. During this period I received a call from the hospital asking if I would go back to see them as the results were showing that the abnormal cells were on the very edge of the sample in the petri dish so they weren't sure if they were mine or not or if there had been any cross contamination. They felt that further investigations were required. I had to go back again for a further biopsy with equipment that was now repaired. I went back for this biopsy and they removed a polyp and it was quite uncomfortable. This wasn't done under a general anaesthetic as I just wanted them to hurry up and get it done as it had been a month now of me not knowing what I had. I received a further phone call within the next two weeks after this to again visit the Consultant and they wouldn't tell me over the phone. The surgeon told me that there were pre-cancerous cells present and this had now been confirmed. She was quite straight forward with me saying that it was most likely that I could have a low grade cancer. I accepted the diagnosis and advised that I would be continuing with my positive affirmations and she said "Good for you but you will need a hysterectomy quite quickly really". I was provided with lots of information about this and was told that they could hopefully perform the operation via keyhole surgery. The Macmillan Nurses came to see me that day at the hospital and I was taken into a room with them. The nurse that I saw that day explained to me that I could call them at any time if I needed to talk about the cancer. I explained that I was so very appreciative of their time but that being a healer I was going to use what I had learnt and work on positive affirmations and use my own healing abilities on myself. I did take their card and thanked them for their offer and explained that it was their reality that I was ill and my reality was that I was not. I felt I couldn't accept anyone else's belief but had to go with my own. Around this time I saw the number 777 many times which means that I am on the right soul path and miracles will happen in my life. So I believed that I would be healed and therefore had no anxiety towards the "C" word. Consequently I was asked to take part in a clinical trial using Metformin a placebo to which I agreed as I felt it may help other people. During this time I decided I wanted to have a medium at my home to provide readings for me and a group of my friends. Ali Mather, the medium, agreed and came to give us all individual sittings. My sitting with her was the last and within minutes of talking to me she said she was picking up problems in my womb area. I told her that I did have a problem and she advised me that I had always been ill in that area and explained it was of the endometrium but she said that it was more than that. I have this all on tape. I told her that I had been diagnosed with pre-cancerous cells of the endometrium. She then went on to tell me that I would be completely healed and that it was fate and it had no reflection on my drinking heavily or anything else that Anthony may have done to me. It was on my destiny pathway and that I was a healer and had to experience this. She advised me that I did need to go through the operation as this was part of the learning process to help others. Ali went on to tell me that I had a healing guide who was there to help me heal and mentioned that I was a vegetarian and she said my guide was Asian and a vegetarian. To cut a long story short I knew in my mind that I was going to be alright. I was listed for the operation which was about a month later.

Lynn, a very kind friend of mine, took me to hospital very early on the morning of the operation. I was a little nervous walking down to the theatre and when they put the anaesthetic in I remember saying to them that my angels were with me and that I would be fine after the operation in all ways. They just looked at me as if I was off another planet really. The team really looked after me though and I am grateful for their skills and compassion. When I woke up from the anaesthetic I did all the breathing exercises and some leg exercises straight away. The following morning I was up and about as soon as I could. I showered and went for a little walk along the ward. I know the process from being a physiotherapist. The Consultant said I had done really well after the operation and that they would be in touch with the next stage of treatment that I would require when the results came through from the tissue removed. I was allowed home that same day and my brother came to pick me up and I stayed with my mum for a few weeks. Interestingly I received lots of cards and flowers because people see cancer as a life threatening illness, however, when I was an alcoholic no one cared less about me as I feel people believe this to be self- inflicted and not worthy of their help. They think that alcoholism is a choice and not an illness when in reality it is an illness. People around me actually looked down on me and showed no empathy towards me. Alcohol abuse kills people just the same as cancer. I felt that when I had cancer those around me showed me love but some of the same people who were around me showed me only disgust with my alcoholism yet I was the same person.

I was called back to the hospital within two weeks of my being sent home and basically the Consultant Surgeon was there to discharge me. I knew on the Friday prior to my appointment that it was all clear as the Macmillan Nurse had telephoned to advise me. However, you don't normally have the surgeon discharge you but she wanted to see me herself. During the appointment the surgeon told me that I didn't have to come back and that she was discharging me but that she wanted to talk to me. She stated that my tissue sample was completely normal and healed and she found nothing which was quite impossible according to her as she had been involved in taking the original samples which showed very clearly the pre-cancerous cells. She asked me how I had done that so I explained to her my belief system and my mediumship and numerology uses. I advised her that it all indicated that everything was positive and that I also believed and said affirmations daily that I was well and healthy. She told me that her mother believed in the same as me and I told her that her mother was very wise. She then went on to ask me if she could write me up as a case study to help other women in the future. I agreed and thanked her and then left.

Healing is now a large part of my life and I know that all my experiences have been part of a learning process for me to enable me to help others. My knowledge is increasing all the time and I am still on a learning pathway and at present I am learning Hypnotherapy as I feel this is of benefit and will be yet another tool for me to help people on their pathways. Something I really enjoy is the spiritual development classes that I attend on a weekly basis and I do many fun things such as "Tea Leaf" readings. Just call me mystic Tyff.

I have started to play tennis again now and enjoy it very much. One really positive thing that I have noticed is that I used to cough every morning when I lived with my ex-husband and now I live on my own that has completely gone. I take no medication for depression now and my moods don't need improving. My general wellbeing is like a flow of energy that I am travelling on. I now feel that I am one with the Universe.

There is only one more change needed and that is to correct the injustice that was carried out against me and I am now fighting for justice in rectifying the previous decisions made about me because of Anthony and Katherine's lies about me in life to all my friends and colleagues but also in Katherine's sworn evidence. I went through all the witness statements at the time and read them thoroughly. It's quite laughable really as they are inconsistent, contradictory, and I now have the evidence to prove that they are lies. I have commenced on my journey for justice and have amassed a great deal of evidence from Laney and Dennis which I have sent to the Professional Body in London and have included all the evidence that I have received from the other areas to prove that the statements given by Katherine were dishonest. Since that time I received emails to advise me of one thing or another but basically they have dismissed the case even with written evidence of Katherine's dishonesty. I believe that they did not wish to reopen the case as it would prove that Katherine had been telling lies. I will continue on my journey for justice to prove that Katherine lied and that she was dishonest with her statements.

I have also tried to get the case reopened where I used to work as I now had significant evidence regarding the lies that Katherine had told about me. I telephoned the hospital and requested a complaints form to enable the case to be reopened as instructed by my solicitor. I explained this to them and they said they would be back in touch with me. I also advised that I had significant witness statements and did not state at that point who they were from. I advised that I knew it was out of the timescale for reopening a case but that a massive miscarriage of justice had been carried out. A week or two later I received a phone call from the original investigating officer and she advised me in no uncertain terms that the case was firmly closed. I told her that I was now in possession of witness statements from my friend and neighbour, and also from Katherine's ex-husband Dennis relating to all her previous relationships and behaviour. I also offered other evidence to her to substantiate that I wasn't drunk going to domestic violence meetings and had received a letter from them to support this. The investigating officer informed me that the case was closed, yet again quite abruptly, and that I should leave Katherine alone to get on with her life and for me to get on with mine. I replied to her advising that I hadn't received justice and was there a time limit on that. She just went on to say to me she was too busy and hung up.

I spoke with Dennis regarding this book and he told me that he was somewhat annoyed with me as Katherine had called him demanding to know what evidence was in the letters that had been given to me by him. He told her where to go but nevertheless he was upset that she had found out and had called him. This could only have happened if the investigating officer at the Health Centre had informed Katherine at work. If Katherine had nothing to worry about why would she be causing upset to Dennis with her demands. Quite unnecessary really as her work place were unwilling to reopen a new investigation. I believe she went into a little panic when she was informed what had been stated in our phone call.

I now continue with my life as a single woman and have not been in a full on relationship for nearly four years now but feel I am ready to move forwards as not all men are like my ex-husband and I was just unlucky and there are wonderful men out there. I won't allow the past to interfere with my future.

I am now involved with numerology and working with the Angels which I love and often see relevant numbers wherever I may go. These are the answers to what I had asked for and it always comes when I need it. I am always respectful and thank the Universe and the Angels for what I have received.
There is one comment that I fully believe in and that is "What goes around comes around and this is called Karma".

My dreams came true because I was willing to put in the time and the effort and I believed I could and would be healed through love, great friends, and my family.

There's a funny story on the internet at the minute and it's very true and it goes like this:

A man is waiting patiently for a car park space when suddenly one becomes available and from nowhere a vehicle rushes into the space before him. The man in this vehicle gets out and tells the patient driver to "F… O…" which amazed him and he thought what a rude ignorant man. The patient man finally gets into a parking space and makes his way to work as he is a job interviewer. Guess who the applicant was? Guess who didn't get the job? This is called instant Karma. I know lots of stories like this and I truly believe it is true.

I truly believe that Karma will arrive for Anthony and Katherine when they least expect it.

I just wanted to tell you about a rice experiment that was carried out by a doctor by putting some rice in three glass beakers and covering the rice in each beaker with water. Then every day for a month the doctor said thank you to the first beaker, the second one he said you're an idiot and the last beaker he completely ignored. After one month the rice that had been thanked had begun to ferment giving off a pleasant aroma, the rice in the second beaker turned black and the rice in the third was rotting. The doctor believes that as children and adults what we are told can either cause harm or be of benefit to us. However, being ignored is worse.

I was told by Anthony over a prolonged period of twenty years that I was a useless piece of shit and that I wasn't capable of doing anything properly or I was constantly told I was an unfit mother. He told me I was fat and lazy. I can't really remember him saying anything positive to me during my years with him. So eventually I became to believe this and lost all my self-esteem and confidence when near him or in the home. I was fine at work because I always received positive words with regard to my work and capabilities. Then that changed as my home life impacted on my work life. As people we absorb all the words spoken to us and assimilate them into our mind accordingly as the harmful messages enter the subconscious mind and then become our reality. The subconscious doesn't know whether what is being received is real or not so therapy can bring about the changes with our thinking processes.

# Afterword

The day I released myself from Anthony was the first day of my new beginnings as I no longer needed his approval and control in my life. Moving into a more spiritual place in my life brought the new beginnings I desperately needed and I regained my self-respect and self-esteem and was now able to control my life myself. I took control of my life and then gained more and more knowledge and now I have a thirst for knowledge and am on a new pathway in a very different direction than I was previously.

Every day I had one action step that I would say first thing in the morning and I did this daily. I actually used to say it to my dear old dad. I act on the action steps every day and bring about the changes immediately. Taking one step at a time brought about enormous changes and God does truly help those who help themselves. It's not enough to just wish for something we have to take the action steps to get it or bring it about.

As I had gathered all the evidence needed for my justice to come about, the Universe could then provide the help I needed and it truly did. There is one thing that I always have and that is trust and faith that it will all turn out for the best in the end.

My life has been a transformation from a butterfly into a chrysalis then back into a butterfly again and I send my thanks to the Universe for helping me by sending all the people I needed into my life. I am so lucky because the statistics of recovery from alcoholism is only about three per cent and I am one of those. People label alcoholics for the rest of their lives and this is unjust. People are unlikely to have the same opinion if someone has been a smoker and given up they don't get labelled. Mr or Mrs Famous alcoholic is often remembered as a character even though they drank to extremes all their lives yet Mr or Mrs Joe

Public are often judged more harshly and they may have experienced a much harder life.

Alcoholics are, in the main, treated as socially unacceptable and I can say this through my own personal experience. The difference for me was that I was so lucky and grateful to have an extremely supportive loving family and some truly marvellous friends that I had during the bad times and that are still with me today. All the others dropped me like a tonne of bricks. I was treated like a leper by the majority of the people in my life.

I am now proud of who I am and what I am.

# The Co-Authors

Laney Pemberton and I have co-written this book together. It is our first book and Laney is already on her second book a true chilling paranormal story and we are now both working together again on a fictional story.

Laney Pemberton is a qualified business tutor and has reached the top of her career tree only to find that it wasn't what she wanted. She then went on a spiritual journey and the gift she put to one side from being a child developed into her physic abilities and her mediumship over a period of thirty years. Laney is also a healer and tutors others to develop their mediumistic and psychic gifts. She never liked school but excelled over the twenty years after school obtaining many qualifications. Laney has a very happy life in her cottage with her partner, his two sons, three cats, dog and fish in her outside pond and inside aquariums, on the West Pennine Moors surrounded by nature. She didn't like life in semi-suburbia with the wrong man in her life and now she has a wonderful man in her life and is living her dreams.

Laney is a light worker and was Tyff's friend before she met her husband and has now rekindled her friendship of many years with Tyff.

Tyff has told the story of her life which is where the title came from by Laney that Life Hurts but Only Sometimes. Tyff has many qualifications in the academic side of life but her main sole purpose and mission is using her healing abilities to benefit others. Tyff was a qualified physiotherapist in the community. She actively practices her healing abilities and is often asked to use this gift whilst doing a massage for her clients. Her next mission is to set up a group for people on social media to bridge the gap from diagnosis of illness through the healing pathway. She is able to help people through their emotional journeys as she has completed this process herself. Tyff is also a light worker and has learnt many lessons on her traumatic and emotional journey to where she is today. Tyff lives in her own home in Manchester, close to nature, near water and near meadows. Tyff had a wonderful happy childhood and her favourite place was a tree den in the woods surrounded by nature and a beautiful stream. She spent all her time believing in fairies, angels and being a princess and she lived this life as a child. In her school report it stated that Tyff lived in a world of castles, princesses, fairies and dreams. The teacher then put that she was a very happy child and academically bright. She took all the lead roles with her creativity in all the school plays she was Puck in Midsummers Night Dream, and the Sorcerer in The Sorcerer's Apprentice.

# The publisher

*He who stops
getting better
stops being good.*

This is the motto of novum publishing, and our focus
is on finding new manuscripts, publishing them and
offering long-term support to the authors.
Our publishing house was founded in 1997, and since
then it has become THE expert for new authors and
has won numerous awards.

**Our editorial team will peruse each manuscript
within a few weeks free of charge and without
obligation.**

You will find more information about
novum publishing and our books on the internet:

w w w . n o v u m - p u b l i s h i n g . c o . u k